An Analysis of

David Hume's

Dialogues Concerning Natural Religion

John Donaldson
With
Ian Jackson

Published by Macat International Ltd
24:13 Coda Centre, 189 Munster Road, London SW6 6AW.

Distributed exclusively by Routledge
2 Park Square, Milton Park, Abingdon, Oxon OX14 4RN
711 Third Avenue, New York, NY 10017, USA

Routledge is an imprint of the Taylor & Francis Group, an informa business

www.macat.com
info@macat.com

Cataloguing in Publication Data
A catalogue record for this book is available from the British Library.
Library of Congress Cataloguing-in-Publication Data is available upon request.
Cover illustration: A. Richard Allen

ISBN 978-1-912303-00-7 (hardback)
ISBN 978-1-912128-95-2 (paperback)
ISBN 978-1-912281-88-6 (e-book)

Notice
The information in this book is designed to orientate readers of the work under analysis,
to elucidate and contextualise its key ideas and themes, and to aid in the development
of critical thinking skills. It is not meant to be used, nor should it be used, as a
substitute for original thinking or in place of original writing or research. References and
notes are provided for informational purposes and their presence does not constitute
endorsement of the information or opinions therein. This book is presented solely for
educational purposes. It is sold on the understanding that the publisher is not engaged
to provide any scholarly advice. The publisher has made every effort to ensure that
this book is accurate and up-to-date, but makes no warranties or representations with
regard to the completeness or reliability of the information it contains. The information
and the opinions provided herein are not guaranteed or warranted to produce particular
results and may not be suitable for students of every ability. The publisher shall not be
liable for any loss, damage or disruption arising from any errors or omissions, or from
the use of this book, including, but not limited to, special, incidental, consequential or
other damages caused, or alleged to have been caused, directly or indirectly, by the
information contained within.

CONTENTS

WAYS IN TO THE TEXT

Who Was David Hume? 9

What Does *Dialogues Concerning Natural Religion* Say? 10

Why Does *Dialogues Concerning Natural Religion* Matter? 12

SECTION 1: INFLUENCES

Module 1: The Author and the Historical Context 15

Module 2: Academic Context 20

Module 3: The Problem 24

Module 4: The Author's Contribution 29

SECTION 2: IDEAS

Module 5: Main Ideas 34

Module 6: Secondary Ideas 39

Module 7: Achievement 43

Module 8: Place in the Author's Work 48

SECTION 3: IMPACT

Module 9: The First Responses 53

Module 10: The Evolving Debate 58

Module 11: Impact and Influence Today 63

Module 12: Where Next? 67

Glossary of Terms 72

People Mentioned in the Text 79

Works Cited 86

THE MACAT LIBRARY

The Macat Library is a series of unique academic explorations of seminal works in the humanities and social sciences – books and papers that have had a significant and widely recognised impact on their disciplines. It has been created to serve as much more than just a summary of what lies between the covers of a great book. It illuminates and explores the influences on, ideas of, and impact of that book. Our goal is to offer a learning resource that encourages critical thinking and fosters a better, deeper understanding of important ideas.

Each publication is divided into three Sections: Influences, Ideas, and Impact. Each Section has four Modules. These explore every important facet of the work, and the responses to it.

This Section-Module structure makes a Macat Library book easy to use, but it has another important feature. Because each Macat book is written to the same format, it is possible (and encouraged!) to cross-reference multiple Macat books along the same lines of inquiry or research. This allows the reader to open up interesting interdisciplinary pathways.

To further aid your reading, lists of glossary terms and people mentioned are included at the end of this book (these are indicated by an asterisk [*] throughout) – as well as a list of works cited.

Macat has worked with the University of Cambridge to identify the elements of critical thinking and understand the ways in which six different skills combine to enable effective thinking.
Three allow us to fully understand a problem; three more give us the tools to solve it. Together, these six skills make up the **PACIER** model of critical thinking. They are:

ANALYSIS – understanding how an argument is built
EVALUATION – exploring the strengths and weaknesses of an argument
INTERPRETATION – understanding issues of meaning

CREATIVE THINKING – coming up with new ideas and fresh connections
PROBLEM-SOLVING – producing strong solutions
REASONING – creating strong arguments

To find out more, visit **WWW.MACAT.COM.**

CRITICAL THINKING AND *DIALOGUES CONCERNING NATURAL RELIGION*

Primary critical thinking skill: REASONING
Secondary critical thinking skill: EVALUATION

David Hume's *Dialogues Concerning Natural Religion* is a philosophical classic that displays a powerful mastery of the critical thinking skills of reasoning and evaluation.

Hume's subject, the question of the existence and possible nature of God, was, and still is, a persistent topic of philosophical and theological debate. What makes Hume's text a classic of reasoning, though, is less what he says, than how he says it. As he noted in his preface to the book, the question of 'natural religion' was unanswerable: so 'obscure and uncertain' that 'human reason can reach no fixed determination with regard to it.'

Hume chose, as a result, to cast his thoughts on the topic in the form of a dialogue – allowing different points of view to be reasoned out, evaluated and answered by different characters. Considering and judging different or opposing points of view, as Hume's characters do, is an important part of reasoning, and is vital to building strong persuasive arguments. Even if, as Hume suggests, there can be no final answer to what a god might be like, *Dialogues Concerning Natural Religion* shows high-level reasoning and evaluation at their best.

ABOUT THE AUTHOR OF THE ORIGINAL WORK

Born in Edinburgh, Scotland in 1711, the brilliant **David Hume** entered the University of Edinburgh at the age of 12, seemingly destined for a career in academia. But his religious views put him outside the intellectual mainstream. Hume was skeptical of Christianity and arguably did not believe in God. So he became a diplomat and writer, establishing a reputation as one of the finest thinkers of his generation. That reputation has endured: many believe Hume was the greatest philosopher ever to write in English.

ABOUT THE AUTHORS OF THE ANALYSIS

Dr John Donaldson holds a PhD in philosophy from the University of Glasgow, where he now teaches. His work focuses on philosophy of mind, particularly the metaphysics of mind: the problem of mental causation, the mind-body problem, and the prospects for materialist accounts of mental phenomena.

Ian Jackson is a PhD student in the Politics, Philosophy and Religion department at Lancaster University. He is interested in the role new media plays in the dissemination of ideas.

ABOUT MACAT

GREAT WORKS FOR CRITICAL THINKING

Macat is focused on making the ideas of the world's great thinkers accessible and comprehensible to everybody, everywhere, in ways that promote the development of enhanced critical thinking skills.

It works with leading academics from the world's top universities to produce new analyses that focus on the ideas and the impact of the most influential works ever written across a wide variety of academic disciplines. Each of the works that sit at the heart of its growing library is an enduring example of great thinking. But by setting them in context – and looking at the influences that shaped their authors, as well as the responses they provoked – Macat encourages readers to look at these classics and game-changers with fresh eyes. Readers learn to think, engage and challenge their ideas, rather than simply accepting them.

'Macat offers an amazing first-of-its-kind tool for
interdisciplinary learning and research. Its focus on works
that transformed their disciplines and its rigorous approach,
drawing on the world's leading experts and educational institutions,
opens up a world-class education to anyone.'

Andreas Schleicher
Director for Education and Skills, Organisation for Economic
Co-operation and Development

'Macat is taking on some of the major challenges in university
education ... They have drawn together a strong team of active
academics who are producing teaching materials that are
novel in the breadth of their approach.'

Prof Lord Broers,
former Vice-Chancellor of the University of Cambridge

'The Macat vision is exceptionally exciting. It focuses
upon new modes of learning which analyse and explain seminal texts
which have profoundly influenced world thinking and so social and
economic development. It promotes the kind of critical thinking
which is essential for any society and economy.
This is the learning of the future.'

Rt Hon Charles Clarke, former UK Secretary of State for Education

'The Macat analyses provide immediate access to the critical
conversation surrounding the books that have shaped their
respective discipline, which will make them an invaluable resource
to all of those, students and teachers, working in the field.'

Professor William Tronzo, University of California at San Diego

WAYS IN TO THE TEXT

KEY POINTS

- One of the leading figures of the period of European cultural history known as the Enlightenment*—a time characterized by a turn toward rationality and science—David Hume (1711–76) is often considered the greatest philosopher to have written in the English language.

- In *Dialogues Concerning Natural Religion*, Hume grapples with how to justify belief in God—and what is even meant by "God."

- Hume presents his arguments as a dialogue*—a dramatic narrative where the reader's thinking is guided by the thoughts and words of different characters—without explicitly revealing his own views.

Who Was David Hume?

David Hume, the author of *Dialogues Concerning Natural Religion* (published in 1779), was born in 1711 in the Scottish capital, Edinburgh. The second son of socially advantaged (if not wealthy) parents, he was a gifted child who studied at the University of Edinburgh from the age of 11 or 12. He went on to become a central figure in the Enlightenment.[1] In this period, roughly between 1600 and 1800, advances in science and philosophy radically influenced European society and culture; superstition and religious belief were challenged by an emphasis on rational thought.

Although highly regarded by fellow intellectuals, Hume often clashed with the more conservative forces of eighteenth-century Scotland. This struggle with the defenders of tradition defined his life. Often at odds with prominent conservative churchmen, Hume did not hide his opinion of such conservatism in his work. On account of the notoriety this brought, Hume found himself denied any truly prestigious academic post. He found obvious career success in other areas, though, being appointed secretary to the British embassy in Paris, for example.

Following his death in 1776 it took some time before he became recognized as an important philosopher. This happened in part because of the influence his thinking had on the highly influential German philosopher Immanuel Kant,* particularly noticeable in Kant's *Critique of Pure Reason* (1781) and *Prolegomena* (1783). But before this important endorsement, Hume was mainly thought of as a successful historian and an accomplished writer and, if anything, as a philosopher of middling importance. Today, however, he is widely recognized as the greatest philosopher ever to have written in English.[2]

What Does *Dialogues Concerning Natural Religion* say?

Dialogues could hardly have a more controversial subject—belief in the existence of God. Although Hume completed the first draft in 1751, his friends, worried that the book's ideas were too provocative, dissuaded him from publishing it.[3]

Hume took great pains to write *Dialogues* in a way that would shield it from the kind of outrage that might drown out his arguments, saying to his friend the economist and philosopher Adam Smith* that "nothing can be more cautiously and more artfully written."[4]

This partly accounts for why Hume wrote the book as a dialogue—a dramatic narrative in which characters discuss weighty ideas. It allows Hume to lead readers toward conclusions they might not otherwise be able to accept. Blasphemy—speaking sacrilegiously about God—was a serious criminal offense at the time, and Hume was very concerned about such a charge being brought against him. Perhaps as a result of this, his approach to *Dialogues* was so subtle it led to disagreement over what Hume was actually saying.

Scholars tend to agree, though, that *Dialogues* reflects Hume's low regard for organized religion, particularly where clerical influence in society is concerned.[5] And any arguments allowing for a belief in God that Hume is sympathetic to are so far removed from religious orthodoxy as to call into question whether the term "God" should be used at all.[6]

One of the text's clearest conclusions is that the question of God's existence should be examined *empirically*.* According to empiricist* thought, the ultimate source of all knowledge is what can be verified by observation.

Dialogues, then, is a defense of the empiricist method and is based on a type of *natural theology*.* Natural theology is founded on the principle that claims about religion have to be justified by a rational argument, rather than by the words of any religious authority or text alone. This is why Hume uses the phrase "natural religion"* in the title of his book, invoking the idea that God and all aspects of the supernatural are part of nature.

Hume tackles four main arguments about God's existence.

- *The argument from design** (also known as the *teleological argument*),* supporting the idea of belief in God by pointing to there being design, or planning, in nature.
- *The cosmological argument,** which supports a belief in God by maintaining that the universe must have an uncaused first cause; this means something must have caused the universe to exist—a cause which can only be God.
- *The argument from evil,** which weighs against God's existence simply because there is evil in the world.
- The debate about whether God's nature is *knowable*, and if it is, what that nature is.

Dialogues is a literary and philosophical masterpiece that is still extremely relevant today. The book investigates the ongoing battle across the world between two different sets of cultural values, the traditional and the progressive. The constant struggle between conservative and liberal world views is as visible today as it was in Hume's eighteenth century, and the subtle arguments laid out in *Dialogues* are still useful as we try to understand it.

Why Does *Dialogues Concerning Natural Religion* Matter?

Across the world people argue, fight, and die over how we should live in order to please God. Religiously-motivated violence occurs on every continent, inspired by many different religions; conflicts between different religions or sects routinely have implications far beyond the specific site of the conflict itself.

Religion also provokes a great deal of more peaceful debate, including over, for example, the role of faith schools in state education, and whether belief should be allowed to guide doctors who oppose abortion, or bakers who refuse to make wedding cakes for gay couples. In the United States the conversation continues over evolution and intelligent design* (the idea that the complexity and apparent perfection of the constitution of plants and animals somehow proves the existence of a divine "designer") and how science should be taught in schools. Intelligent design came about as a result of restrictions on the teaching of religion in schools; it was an unsuccessful attempt to create a scientific theory that included the concept of a creator.

So a masterpiece that takes us to the very heart of this matter can only help us make sense of the many issues around belief in God. To our modern minds, eighteenth-century circles may seem more well-mannered than our own. However, Hume was right at the center of this heated debate over the nature and existence of God. His ideas in *Dialogues* were so outrageous for religious people in his own age that Hume would not allow them to be published until he was safely dead.

This is in many ways understandable, because he leads us to confront a famously huge question: Is there a God?

Hume had to use every persuasive device at his disposal to sway his reader, and to protect himself against the backlash he expected. The result is a masterclass in the "Socratic method,"* named for the ancient Greek philosopher Socrates;* according to this method, participants in a debate ask and answer questions as a way to test the clarity and consistency of their positions. But the most important Socratic exchange that occurs is not between the main characters. It is between Hume and his reader.

If Hume's *Dialogues* still matters after more than two centuries, it is perhaps because the arguments the great thinker took such time to prepare have never been bettered—or, more importantly, overturned.

NOTES

1 See Terence Penelhum, *David Hume: An Introduction to his Philosophical System* (West Lafayette: Purdue University Press, 1992), ix. See also William Edward Morris and Charlotte R. Brown, "David Hume," in *The Stanford Encyclopedia of Philosophy*, ed. Edward N. Zalta (Stanford: Metaphysics Research Lab CSLI, 2014), http://plato.stanford.edu/archives/sum2014/entries/hume/.

2 See Morris and Brown, "David Hume."

3 See Dorothy Coleman (Ed.), "Introduction," in *Hume: Dialogues Concerning Natural Religion and Other Writings* (Cambridge: Cambridge University Press, 2007), xiv.

4 David Hume, "To Adam Smith," in *The Letters of David Hume*, vol. II, ed. J. Y. T. Greig (Oxford: Clarendon Press, 1932), 334.

5 See J. C. A. Gaskin, "Hume on Religion," in *The Cambridge Companion to Hume*, ed. David Fate Norton (Cambridge: Cambridge University Press, 1993), 340–1. See also Andrew Pyle, *Hume's Dialogues Concerning Natural Religion* (London: Continuum, 2006), 122.

6 See Gaskin, "Hume on Religion," 320–2. See also Morris and Brown, "David Hume," 8.4.

SECTION 1
INFLUENCES

MODULE 1
THE AUTHOR AND THE
HISTORICAL CONTEXT

KEY POINTS

- *Dialogues Concerning Natural Religion* is a literary and philosophical masterpiece that tackles the very nature of God.

- Hume had a strict religious upbringing but abandoned his belief as an adult—choosing to release his controversial *Dialogues* only after his death.

- The fierce struggle between the forces of tradition and progress during the Enlightenment* shaped, and was shaped by, this landmark text.

Why Read This Text?

David Hume's *Dialogues Concerning Natural Religion* (1779) is a philosophical masterpiece. Hume's profound and complex mission is to question belief in God; his artfully constructed debate contains what many see as the decisive argument against a designed universe. As Simon Blackburn states, "The great thing about the *Dialogues* is the attack on the argument [from] design, it's usually taken to be the decisive destruction of that argument."[1]

There is also literary beauty in *Dialogues*, which Hume worked on for many years. The arguments are finely wrought in prose to create a great tapestry of reason. Consider the following passage in support of the argument that if evil exists, then God cannot.

"Observe … the curious artifices of Nature, in order to embitter the life of every living being. The stronger prey upon the weaker, and keep them in perpetual terror and anxiety. The weaker too, in their

> **" Hume is our Politics, Hume is our Trade, Hume is our Philosophy, Hume is our Religion. "**
> James Hutchison Stirling, *The Secret of Hegel*

turn, often prey upon the stronger, and vex and molest them without relaxation … And thus on each hand, before and behind, above and below, every animal is surrounded with enemies, which incessantly seek his misery and destruction."[2]

Here we see Hume's signature style at work on how the apparent cruelty and mercilessness of the natural order counts against the existence of an all-powerful, all-knowing, and perfectly good deity. What kind of supreme being would create such a world? There are many examples of profound ideas crafted in high literary style in *Dialogues*. The philosophical depth and literary beauty of the text has ensured its status as of one the most influential texts in the philosophy of religion.

Author's Life

Hume was born in the Scottish city of Edinburgh in 1711 to Joseph and Katherine Home (pronounced "Hume"; as an adult he adopted the phonetic spelling). He was only two when his father, a lawyer, died. He was raised by his mother and was such an intellectually gifted child that when his older brother went to study at the University of Edinburgh, Hume went with him, even though he was at the most 12 years old. The usual age for going to university at the time was 14. Hume studied Latin and Greek but read widely in literature, history, philosophy, and natural science, and soon decided to pursue the life of a scholar and philosopher. He never graduated, however, possibly because he thought his teachers were useless.

As a young man, Hume abandoned the religious beliefs of his strict Calvinist* upbringing, though he drew back from expressing his

criticisms in print (Calvinism is a notably austere sect of the Protestant*
branch of Christianity). He removed, for example, a critical discussion
of miracles before publishing his first work, *A Treatise of Human Nature*
(1738–40). Although he held high hopes for the work, in his view "it
fell *dead-born from the press*; without reaching such distinction as even to
excite a Murmur among the Zealots."[3] This was an overly pessimistic
assessment. The *Treatise* caused sufficient excitement "among the
Zealots" (conservative clergy) for Hume to be refused an academic
chair at both Edinburgh and Glasgow universities, in 1745 and 1752,
respectively (although by the time he was refused the Glasgow chair,
Hume had also published *An Enquiry Concerning Human Understanding*,
which built on much of the material in the *Treatise*). At this time, a
reputation as an atheist* was a serious bar to holding an academic post.

Hume found great success as a historian, however, with his *History
of England* (published in six volumes between 1754 and 1762). It was a
best seller for many years, providing him with financial security and
independence.

Hume never felt comfortable expressing his views on religion in
print at a time when controversial views on religious matters could
lead to serious repercussions. Throughout his life he was persuaded to
hold back from publishing controversial material.[4] None was
considered more controversial than *Dialogues Concerning Natural
Religion*. Eventually Hume decided his incendiary ideas should be
published after he died—which they were, in 1779.

They provided his final thoughts on his most ambitious project—a
discussion of the nature and existence of God.

Author's Background

Scotland in the eighteenth century was at the forefront of the
Enlightenment,* a period in which science and philosophy flourished
as thinkers used reason to challenge traditional beliefs. Hume is among
a number of prominent figures, including the philosopher Francis

Hutcheson,* the foundational economist Adam Smith,* the philosopher Thomas Reid,* and the influential social theorist Adam Ferguson,* whose contributions to the era were so significant that their ideas make up what is known as the Scottish Enlightenment.[5] Although its role in public life was increasingly questioned, religion was a powerful force in Scottish society in the eighteenth century. Scots were becoming increasingly literate, their education system was expanding, and the wider social and intellectual forces of the Enlightenment were being felt. As human knowledge advanced in Europe, religion began a slow retreat; at this time, that retreat was mostly to be found in academic circles.

A caricature of the period might paint a simplistic picture of opposing forces—religion against science, faith against reason, regression against progress. The reality was much more complex, however. In *Dialogues* Hume shows how different arguments cut across one another to create an intricate debate. Key elements included the opposition between empiricism* (knowledge based on observation) and rationalism* (knowledge based on reason) and the opposition between an understanding of God through revealed theology* (that is, in revelations and texts) and an understanding based on natural theology* (that is, in terms of the natural world).

Hume directed his writing at fellow members of the intelligentsia*—the intellectual class. He was well connected among intellectuals and had friends on both sides of these debates. He also wanted to engage with the wider educated population.

NOTES

1   See Simon Blackburn, interview by Nigel Warburton, *fivebooks.com*, July 8, 2013, http://fivebooks.com/interviews/simon-blackburn-on-david-hume.

2   David Hume, *Dialogues Concerning Natural Religion*, ed. Stanley Tweyman (London, Routledge, 1991), 153.

3   David Hume, "My Own Life," in *The Letters of David Hume*, vol. I, ed. J. Y. T. Greig (Oxford: Clarendon Press, 1932), 2.

4   Dorothy Coleman (Ed.), "Introduction," in *Hume: Dialogues Concerning Natural Religion and Other Writings* (Cambridge: Cambridge University Press, 2007), XIV.

5   See Alexander Broadie, "Scottish Philosophy in the 18th Century," in *The Stanford Encyclopedia of Philosophy,* ed. Edward N. Zalta (Stanford: Metaphysics *Research Lab CSLI,* 2013), http://plato.stanford.edu/archives/fall2013/entries/scottish-18th/.

MODULE 2
ACADEMIC CONTEXT

KEY POINTS

- Philosophy of religion investigates the foundations of religious thought, particularly claims about the existence of God.

- This means asking how we can understand the nature of God and whether such a God exists.

- According to Hume, knowledge should be based on the evidence of our senses—meaning that there are major problems with every position one might hold on God.

The Work in its Context

Two major philosophical debates are key to understanding David Hume's *Dialogues Concerning Natural Religion*. The first debate is between empiricism* (the view that we gain knowledge through sensory experience) and rationalism* (the view that we gain at least some knowledge independently of our sensory experience). The other is between natural theology* (the belief that religious claims must be justified by rational argument) and revealed theology* (the belief that religious belief is justified because a religious authority or text says something).

Rationalists disagree with empiricists about many things, but especially over the answer to this question of the source of knowledge. For rationalists, we know at least some things independently of sensory experience (that is, without seeing, hearing, touching, smelling, or tasting the evidence). Their favorite example is mathematics, which we know only through reasoning and theoretical deduction—a kind of knowledge known as "a priori"* (a Latin phrase meaning "from the earlier").

❝ Generally speaking, the errors in religion are dangerous; those in philosophy only ridiculous. **❞**
David Hume, *A Treatise of Human Nature*

Empiricists deny this, and say that all knowledge is based on sensory experience.[1] For them, while pure mathematics does not require verification through the senses, without the senses it would never have occurred to us to conceptualize mathematics in the first place.

This general debate has important implications for questions about the existence of God. How does anyone establish that God exists? Empirically, through sensory experience? Or is it a priori knowledge arrived at through reason? Hume, the arch empiricist, argues that any justification has to be empirical. The intense debate continues to this day.[2]

There are two camps in natural theology. For one, claims about God can be made according to reason and deduction; for the other, they must be made empirically. Those who favor revealed theology, on the other hand, say claims about God should be justified in a different way altogether. They should rely on an appeal to special experiences (religious revelations) or texts with sacred content.

Overview of the Field

Philosophy of religion asks many metaphysical questions, notably about the existence of God. Metaphysics* is the area of philosophy that investigates things such as space, time, knowing, and so on—the fundamental things that together constitute reality. A major part of metaphysics is ontology*—inquiry into the nature of being. The question "Does God exist?" is, then, both an ontological and a metaphysical question.

Empiricism is based on one core idea—that all we can rely on when it comes to understanding the world is what we gain through our senses.

This requires us to ask questions about metaphysics itself and leaves empiricists with two main options.

The first is to argue that the supposedly a priori propositions of metaphysics (those supposedly based on reason and deduction) are actually empirical (based on evidence verifiable by observation). The second is to consider as meaningless all those metaphysical propositions that cannot be guaranteed as true by observation.

To opt for this second option is to choose an empiricist theory of meaning.[3]

Empiricists, then, have these two options when considering the existence of God. To argue that God exists, they must use the resources of the empiricist wing of natural theology. That means appealing to arguments such as the argument from design*—the universe appears designed so it must have a designer. An empiricist out to deny that God exists has to contest such arguments. Much of *Dialogues* is concerned with precisely this clash. The book also ponders whether anyone should even try to settle the issue of God's existence empirically.

These debates cannot be properly understood without grasping the wider dispute that underpins them—the dispute, that is, considering the truth and scope of empiricism as a theory of knowledge and meaning.

Academic Influences

The empiricist tradition was a major influence on Hume, who followed closely in the footsteps of fellow philosophers John Locke* of England and George Berkeley of Ireland.* Together they are the central figures of the school known as British empiricism.*

Hume is probably the greatest empiricist of the modern period, not just because of his status as a philosopher, but also because he was, in this regard, a purist. In his view, earlier varieties of empiricism had been "tinged with a metaphysical necessitarianism which was repugnant to Hume's way of thinking"[4] ("necessitarianism" here refers to the philosophical position that one thing causes another, and that there is no other way for reality to be than the state in which we observe it).

Dialogues provides a good indication of just how strident Hume's thinking was. The following famous passage, taken from his *Enquiry Concerning Human Understanding*, is perhaps the best example of his attitude.[5] "When we run over libraries, persuaded of these principles, what havoc must we make? If we take in our hand any volume; of divinity or school metaphysics, for instance; let us ask, *Does it contain any abstract reasoning concerning quantity or number?* No. *Does it contain any experimental reasoning concerning matter of fact and existence?* No. Commit it then to the flames: For it can contain nothing but sophistry and illusion."[6]

And in *Dialogues* we find Hume endeavoring to "commit to the flames" much, if not all, of that found in any "volume of divinity." That is much, if not all, of orthodox religious belief.

NOTES

1 This is a simplified picture of the debate. For a more detailed overview, see Peter Markie, "Rationalism vs. Empiricism," in *The Stanford Encyclopedia of Philosophy,* ed. Edward N. Zalta (Stanford: Metaphysics *Research Lab CSLI,* 2015), http://plato.stanford.edu/archives/sum2015/entries/rationalism-empiricism/.

2 David Bourget and David J. Chalmers, "What Do Philosophers Believe?" *Philosophical Studies* 170 (2014): 465–500.

3 Again, this is a simplified picture. For a more detailed overview, see Markie, "Rationalism vs. Empiricism."

4 E. C. Mossner, *The Life of David Hume*, 2nd ed. (Oxford, Oxford University Press, 2001), 486.

5 For an excellent overview of Hume's views on the centrality of empiricism to philosophy, see William Edward Morris and Charlotte R. Brown, "David Hume," in *The Stanford Encyclopedia of Philosophy*, ed. Edward N. Zalta (Stanford: Metaphysics *Research Lab CSLI,* 2014), http://plato.stanford.edu/archives/sum2014/entries/hume/, § 3.

6 David Hume, *An Enquiry Concerning Human Understanding*, ed. Tom L. Beauchamp (Oxford: Oxford University Press, 1999), 211.

MODULE 3
THE PROBLEM

KEY POINTS

- Hume tackles two old and inseparable questions: Does God exist? What method should we use to find out?

- Atheists* claim that God's *non*existence can be established; theists* and deists* (adherents of related perspectives on the nature of God's role in the universe) think God's *existence* can be established; agnostics* disagree with everyone, believing there is no way of truly knowing.

- In *Dialogues Concerning Natural Religion* Hume protects his work from being dismissed as the ideas of a possible atheist by personifying the arguments in three characters.

Core Question

Two overlapping questions lie at the heart of David Hume's *Dialogues Concerning Natural Religion*: Can God's existence or nonexistence be established? What method can be used to find the answer?

In the eighteenth century, as Hume wrote the text, powerful forces (notably the Church) declared the answer to the first question well and truly settled. God certainly did exist as far as most people were concerned. There was less agreement, however, on how to *show* they were right. Defenders of belief in God needed a convincing answer to that second question.

Revealed theology*—the study of sacred texts from the position that their content was revealed to human beings by a divine authority—offered a position on the existence of God that seemed unquestionable, being safe from rational scrutiny. The most radical version of this approach is fideism,* according to which (as the French

> ❝ Is [God] willing to prevent evil, but not able? Then is he impotent. Is he able, but not willing? Then is he malevolent. Is he both able and willing? Whence then is evil? ❞
>
> Epicurus, in David Hume, *Dialogues Concerning Natural Religion*

religious philosopher Blaise Pascal* described it), it is entirely futile to employ reason in questions of belief.

But revealed theology and fideism face big problems. Revelations can be contradictory—so how to distinguish delusion from divinity? In an increasingly secular eighteenth century there was significant pressure on the faithful to defend themselves against the advance of atheism (the position that there is no God) and agnosticism (the position that it is impossible to truly know).

Natural theology* seems to offer a solution. It offers rational arguments in place of appeals to religious experiences or holy books. But that introduces an element of philosophical danger: accepting the need for rational arguments to justify belief in God allows the possibility that the debate might be lost.

The dilemma faced by believers is this: they can either end any participation in rational argument, believing that revealed theology makes it meaningless anyway, and in doing so, let their opponents occupy the field of rational argument unopposed; or they can face those opponents, armed with arguments derived from natural theology, and risk the possibility of defeat.

Conservatives tended to take the first option; those following more progressive principles the second. It is striking how *Dialogues* captures this dispute, personified in two characters—progressive Cleanthes* and conservative Demea.*

The Participants

Although not strictly atheists, the ancient Greek philosopher Epicurus* and the seventeenth-century philosophers Baruch Spinoza* of Holland and Thomas Hobbes* of England were considered the main opponents of orthodox religion in Hume's time.[1]

Epicurus thought the universe was governed by mechanistic processes and that deities had no interest in human affairs, including any form of religious observance.[2] Spinoza held that God *is* nature, making God the totality of entities that make up the universe and the laws that govern them. (To be fair, though, Spinoza's point is complex and there is some dispute about how to read him.)[3] In Spinoza's view, God is not anthropomorphic* (like a person) but the very substance of reality itself. Hobbes held that everything is material,[4] agreeing with Spinoza that this included God.[5] Although each thinker held that there was a God or gods, their idea of the divine was so far removed from the way in which God was understood according to the Christianity of Hume's Scotland as to appear very like atheism.

For those who believed in the existence of God, there were two main schools of thought—theism and deism. Theists believe that God is the all-powerful (omnipotent)*, all-seeing (omniscient),* all-good (omnibenevolent)* eternal creator and sustainer of the universe who intervenes directly in human affairs. Deists, however, view God as an architect rather than a micro-manager. According to deism, although God is the creator of the universe, the universe runs itself perfectly in His absence, and He does not interfere in human history. Deism was perhaps the most intellectually respectable theological position for scholars to take in the Enlightenment period, though there was debate about its compatibility with Christianity.[6]

Agnosticism is the view that we cannot know whether God exists. One possibility discussed in *Dialogues* is that God's nature should be understood as simply *the uncaused cause of the universe.*[7]

The Contemporary Debate

In *Dialogues*, Hume builds on the criticisms of orthodox religious belief presented by Epicurus, Spinoza, Hobbes, and others. For example, he presents sophisticated versions of the argument from evil* (that is, that "the existence of evil rules out the existence of God," a position often attributed to Epicurus).

However, Hume's approach in *Dialogues* is a lot subtler than the approach taken by other scholars. Rather than presenting his own view and defending it, Hume plays his opponents off against each other. For example, much of the *Dialogues* consists of Cleanthes, the liberal theologian, and Demea, the conservative theologian, entirely destroying each other's arguments.

This example illustrates why *Dialogues* is a kind of allegory for the arguments of the day and works on two levels. First, the three main characters represent standard positions on the arguments. These are Cleanthes the liberal, Demea the conservative, and a third character, Philo* the skeptic.* Second, Hume uses the debates of Cleanthes, Demea, and Philo to disguise his mission to persuade the reader. Hume probably did this to ensure that the arguments in *Dialogues* could speak for themselves and not be dismissed simply because they were being put forward by one suspected of being an atheist.

NOTES

1   Dorothy Coleman (Ed.), "Introduction," in *Hume: Dialogues Concerning Natural Religion and Other Writings* (Cambridge: Cambridge University Press, 2007), XIII.

2   James Warren, *Facing Death: Epicurus and His Critics* (Cambridge: Cambridge University Press, 2004), 39. See also David Konstan, "Epicurus," in *The Stanford Encyclopedia of Philosophy,* ed. Edward N. Zalta (Stanford: Metaphysics *Research Lab CSLI,* 2014), http://plato.stanford.edu/archives/sum2014/entries/epicurus/, 3.

3   See Steven Nadler, "Baruch Spinoza," in *The Stanford Encyclopedia of Philosophy,* ed. Edward N. Zalta (Stanford: Metaphysics *Research Lab CSLI,* 2013), http://plato.stanford.edu/archives/fall2013/entries/spinoza/, 2.1.

4   See Thomas Hobbes, *Leviathan*, ed. C. B. Macpherson (London: Penguin Books, 1985), 81.

5   P. Springborg, "Hobbes's Challenge to Descartes, Bramhall and Boyle: A Corporeal God," *British Journal for the History of Philosophy*, 20 (2012): 903–34.

6   Charles Taliaferro, and Elsa J.Marty (eds.), *A Dictionary of Philosophy of Religion* (New York: Continuum, 2010), 60–61.

7   David Hume, *Dialogues Concerning Natural Religion*, ed. Stanley Tweyman (London, Routledge, 1991), 108.

MODULE 4
THE AUTHOR'S CONTRIBUTION

KEY POINTS

- Most commentators agree that Hume did not accept that God, in any orthodox sense, exists.

- The text is held by many to be the greatest use of the dialogue form in philosophy since the works of the ancient Greek philosophers.

- While not the first to express views in such opposition to those of the religious establishment, Hume's elegant critique is among the most definitive.

Author's Aims

David Hume's refusal to state what his aims are in writing *Dialogues Concerning Natural Religion* is simultaneously frustrating and appealing. The reader is required to discover these aims through a close reading of the text, while bearing all his other work in mind.

In *Dialogues*, Hume questioned our very ability to understand God. This, for one commentator, was "the linchpin of Hume's attitude to natural science, to our capacities to predict and control nature, to our confidence in a world lying beyond the immediate reach of current experience, as well as to such problems as those of free will, the causal interaction between mind and matter, the reliability of human testimony, and attempts to argue for God as the cause of the Universe."[1] The implications were clear: from Hume's position we could have "no a priori knowledge of what events can cause other events—no armchair knowledge of the particular causal power of things nor of any general principles of causation."[2]

> **❝** [In] a nutshell ... Hume's position is [that] you can't check out of Hotel Supernatural with any more baggage than you took into it. **❞**
>
> Simon Blackburn, interview by Nigel Warburton, *fivebooks.com*

This arguably reflects the most widely held reading of Hume. If he left any room for belief in the existence of God, it was in a sense so distant and lacking in substance that it removed any force from the claim that such a thing exists. That would radically undermine the influence of religious leaders in society.[3]

Approach

Hume presents his ideas by way of a deft and subtle discussion between three people attempting to make different cases. The book is thought by many to be the greatest example of a dialogue since those written in ancient Greece by Plato,*[4] one of the most influential thinkers in the entire Western tradition of philosophy. Hume chooses this classical form in part as a way to boost his powers of persuasion in the face of entrenched belief.

The author wants the arguments to speak for themselves, independently of his reputation as an atheist. It has been pointed out in recent commentary that Hume is supremely economical. When dealing with religious controversy he is careful not to try for more than he really requires. Hume's clearest and most vociferous criticisms of religion are against Christian doctrines (beliefs concerning a specific region of religious ideas), including belief in miracles. He also attacks the prominent role of clerics in society due to their institutional power. Hume explains such ideas quite plainly in his work.[5] It also seems clear that Hume is unconvinced by mainstream ideas of God as the "super-being"—a notion he mocks in *Dialogues*.[6]

God is a concept greatly reduced by Hume, in comparison to orthodox Christian thought, to the status of the first cause of the universe—a cause about which we know little to nothing. Indeed, it should be noted that while Hume seems to allow such a possibility toward the end of *Dialogues*,[7] this serves as an example of the effectiveness of his device of making the book take the form of a conversation. He concedes an empty victory after winning the arguments that really count. Advertising his position from the outset would have meant instant resistance. Instead Hume allows his great ideas to appear naturally out of the cut and thrust of the debate.

Contribution in Context

How original is *Dialogues*? The central arguments—such as whether the natural world has a designer and how there can be a God if there is evil in the world—were discussed long before Hume was born by luminaries of ancient Greece such as Socrates* (the teacher of Plato), Protagoras,* and even earlier philosophers such as Leucippus.* Theism* (the position that there is a God involved in human affairs), deism* (the position that there is a God with no interest in human affairs), and agnosticism* (the position that we can have no idea whether there is a God or not) had also been the subject of philosophical enquiry. Hume's contribution lies in the extraordinarily sharp and elegant nature of his arguments.

Genuinely novel arguments central to a field of philosophy are relatively rare. What usually happens is that philosophers develop or respond to arguments already in existence. They amend; they clarify; they object. In this regard, Hume's *Dialogues* is a magnificent achievement. Hume marshals the debate with the skill and sophistication of a great philosopher. He sees where the pitfalls are and how the summit of persuasion can be reached. Quite simply, he *argues* brilliantly.

Another key feature of Hume's book is his relentless, focused application of empiricist* principles (principles founded on the position that knowledge can only be gained from the experience of the senses). This can be seen in the way he conducts the debate in terms of empiricist natural theology* (according to which religious ideas and claims could be justified by rational argument). Hume is also careful not to rule in or out more than what good empiricist principles allow. This can be seen in his rejection of a human-like super-being on the one hand, and his somewhat disinterested acknowledgment, on the other, that a certain reduced conception of God is possible.

NOTES

1 Simon Blackburn, *How to Read Hume* (London: Granta Books, 2008), 25.

2 Blackburn, *How to Read Hume*, 25.

3 See J. C. A. Gaskin, "Hume on Religion," in *The Cambridge Companion to Hume*, ed. David Fate Norton (Cambridge: Cambridge University Press, 1993), 340–1. See also Andrew Pyle, *Hume's Dialogues Concerning Natural Religion* (London: Continuum, 2006), 122–32. See also William Edward Morris and Charlotte R. Brown, "David Hume," in *The Stanford Encyclopedia of Philosophy*, ed. Edward N. Zalta (Stanford: Metaphysics *Research Lab CSLI,* 2014), http://plato.stanford.edu/archives/sum2014/entries/hume/, 8.4.

4 Dorothy Coleman (Ed.), "Introduction," in *Hume: Dialogues Concerning Natural Religion and Other Writings* (Cambridge: Cambridge University Press, 2007), xi.

5 See Paul Russell, "Hume on Religion," in *The Stanford Encyclopedia of Philosophy,* ed. Edward N. Zalta (Stanford: Metaphysics *Research Lab CSLI,* 2014), http://plato.stanford.edu/archives/win2014/entries/hume-religion/.

6 See David Hume, *Dialogues Concerning Natural Religion*, ed. Stanley Tweyman (London, Routledge, 1991), 128–32.

7 See Hume, *Dialogues*, 184–5.

SECTION 2
IDEAS

MODULE 5
MAIN IDEAS

KEY POINTS

- In *Dialogues* three characters—Demea, Cleanthes,* and Philo*—argue over belief in God and what "God" is taken to mean.

- Hume seems to conclude that the debate should be settled empirically* and that God, in any traditional sense, does not exist.

- Great themes around the existence of God are presented with all of Hume's characteristic elegance—but are deliberately complex to force readers to grapple with the ideas.

Key Themes

There are three main characters in David Hume's *Dialogues Concerning Natural Religion*, each representing a major position in the God debate.

The first is the traditionally minded Demea.* He holds that it is better to simply have faith in God than to examine his existence through the use of reason. If reasoning is required, however, then it should be a priori* (theoretical deduction). Demea uses the famous "cosmological argument,"* according to which the universe could have come into existence only through an uncaused first cause, which must be God.[1] Demea also defends mysticism*—the view that God's nature is unknowable.[2]

The second character is the more progressively minded Cleanthes, who agrees that God exists but disagrees that this can be demonstrated by a priori reasoning. For Cleanthes, God's existence can be shown using empirical reasoning—that is, through a logical consideration of

> **❝** Whatever exists must have a cause ... of its existence ... in mounting up, therefore, from effects to causes, we must either go on in tracing an infinite succession ... or must at last have some recourse to some ultimate cause, that is *necessarily* existent [but] the first supposition is absurd ... [and] we must, therefore, have recourse to a necessarily existent Being ... There is consequently such a being ... a Deity. **❞**
>
> Demea, in David Hume, *Dialogues Concerning Natural Religion*

what can be observed—a position that makes Cleanthes an empiricist natural theologian.* Cleanthes defends the argument from design.* In this, the natural world appears as if it were designed, pointing to the existence of a designer, pointing to God.[3] Cleanthes also defends anthropomorphism*—the position that God has person-like qualities.[4]

The third character is Philo the skeptic.* While Philo's role in *Dialogues* is complex, he often acts as a kind of "devil's advocate," defending contrary positions for the sake of argument and playing Demea and Cleanthes off against one another. Philo does, however, agree with Cleanthes that God's existence can only be justified empirically. Commentators disagree whether Philo accepts the existence of God.[5] His interventions, however, are nearly always directed at undermining arguments for the existence of God. While he occasionally suggests that he would allow for the existence of something that might be labeled "God," for him this might be best understood as simply "that which is the cause of the universe about which we can know almost nothing."

Toward the end of the *Dialogues*, Philo also champions the "argument from evil,"* according to which the existence of God (in the all-powerful theistic* sense) is inconsistent with the existence of evil in the world.[6] Finally, Philo appears to agree with Demea that God's nature is unknowable—though it is important to remember that by "God," Philo simply means something akin to "the cause of the universe."[7]

In addition to the main characters, Hume introduces an inexperienced youth called Pamphillius as a fourth who, having witnessed the Dialogue, writes to his friend. His conclusion, made with deliberate irony on Hume's part, is that Cleanthes' argument was the strongest.

Exploring the Ideas

The characters all take different positions with regard to the existence and nature of God.

The trio's first topic is where each stands on the matter of natural theology—something on which Philo and Demea can agree, neither believing that the issue of God's existence can be settled through the use of reason. Cleanthes, the natural theologian, poses a dilemma for Philo that seems to clinch the point. Natural science shares the methods of natural philology, Cleanthes argues. So if Philo rejects the arguments of natural theology, he must reject much of natural science.[8]

Cleanthes then puts forward an argument representative of natural theology—the argument from design. The universe appears designed, he argues, which means that it must actually have been designed: the appearance of design is best explained by accepting there is an intelligent designer. If the universe has a designer, then that designer is God. Thus God exists.

Cleanthes claims that everything in nature (the eye, for example) seems to have a function, but Philo urges caution. All that we can know empirically, he suggests, is that *parts* of nature seem design-like. What we cannot infer is that nature as a whole shows evidence of design, because we have no experience to support this; we have not observed all of nature or entire universes being built.[9]

Demea is also unimpressed by the argument from design because it only makes God's existence *probable*, not certain. He tries to rectify this situation by presenting the cosmological argument.[10] This is an a priori argument (an argument founded on the use of reason) for the existence of God.[11] The universe has an ultimate cause, the argument goes, since it exists, and if it exists, something must necessarily have created it. This must necessarily have been God.

This argument draws on notions of *necessity* and *contingency*. If *x* exists *contingently*, it means that *x* exists but might not have.

In contrast, if *x* exists *necessarily*, then *x* *must* exist. There is no possible state of affairs in which *x* does not exist.

In plainer terms, this forms part of a classic circular argument where having stated that the existence of the universe is evidence that someone or something created it, we arrive back at the logical conclusion that the creator too must need a creator.

It does not make sense to suggest a contingent entity as the cause of the universe because then you have to ask where that contingent entity came from. Suggesting a necessary entity gets round the problem and stops the argument stretching endlessly backwards.

In Cleanthes' most forceful objection to the cosmological argument, he questions why we should accept that the necessary entity must be God,[12] particularly if the God in question is a substantial one, such as the theistic or deistic* God who may be all-powerful and take an active role in human affairs. Demea's appeal to the cosmological argument brings to mind the thought of the Dutch philosopher Baruch Spinoza,* who takes "God" to refer to nature itself.[13] This is a sense of "God" so far removed from widespread religious teaching that it calls into question whether the use of the term is legitimate.

Language and Expression

Dialogues is written with Hume's trademark wit and verve. The complexity of the debate, and the elaborate, archaic prose can, however, present challenges to the modern reader. The work was aimed at a highly educated eighteenth-century audience and Hume deliberately set out to provoke and perplex, wanting to force people to think deeply about important ideas.

Hume avoids the austere scientific prose typical of much of the philosophy of the period, instead presenting arguments in the form of an animated conversation. This conversation employs metaphor, exaggeration, exclamation, and a number of literary devices. While this adds color, it can also obscure some of the logic and make it difficult to follow the direction of the debate.

Consequently, it is possible to come away from *Dialogues* feeling confused—even confounded. This is not necessarily a bad thing, however; to a large degree, philosophy is a question of the process of working through confusion to achieve clarity of understanding.

NOTES

1   David Hume, *Dialogues Concerning Natural Religion*, ed. Stanley Tweyman (London, Routledge, 1991), 148–51.

2   Hume, *Dialogues*, 107–16.

3   Hume, *Dialogues*, 128–47.

4   Hume, *Dialogues*, 107–16.

5   See Andrew Pyle, *Hume's Dialogues Concerning Natural Religion* (London: Continuum, 2006), 122–32.

6   Hume, *Dialogues*, 152–71.

7   Hume, *Dialogues*, 107–16.

8   Hume, *Dialogues*, 97–106.

9   Hume, *Dialogues*, 107–16.

10 Hume, *Dialogues*, 148–51.

11 This version, at least. There are many versions; for an overview, see Bruce Reichenbach, "Cosmological Argument," in *The Stanford Encyclopedia of Philosophy,* ed. Edward N. Zalta (Stanford: Metaphysics *Research Lab CSLI,* 2013), http://plato.stanford.edu/archives/spr2013/entries/cosmological-argument/.

12 Hume, *Dialogues*, 148–51.

13 Richard Mason, *The God of Spinoza: A Philosophical Study* (Cambridge, Cambridge University Press, 2010), 3.

MODULE 6
SECONDARY IDEAS

KEY POINTS

- The text's characters debate whether God is so mysterious that we can know nothing about his nature, or whether God is a super-person with emotions, beliefs, and desires.

- This clash between mysticism* (the position that God's mystical nature makes him unknowable) and anthropomorphism* (the position that we can consider God to be human-like), an important part of *Dialogues*, cuts across the other debates in interesting ways.

- The arguments around an unknowable versus a human-like "God" and how the existence of evil in the world can be understood are major issues in their own right within the philosophy of religion.

Other Ideas

David Hume's *Dialogues Concerning Natural Religion* offers a discussion on both the existence and the nature of God. Is God utterly unknowable by virtue of his supernatural nature? Or does he have human-like ways (an anthropomorphic understanding of the Supreme Being)?

Demea,* who subscribes to a mystical understanding of God, opens the debate by defending the position that his nature is unknowable. As he states: "The question is not concerning the being, but the Nature of God. This, I affirm, from the infirmities of human understanding, to be altogether incomprehensible and unknown to us. The essence of that supreme mind, his attributes, the manner of his existence, the very nature of his duration; these and every particular, which regards so divine a being, are mysterious to men."[1] Even to question God's existence is sacrilege to Demea.

> ❝ [How] do you *mystics*, who maintain the absolute incomprehensibility of the deity, differ from sceptics* or atheists, who assert that the first cause of all is unknown and unintelligible? ❞
>
> Cleanthes to Demea, in David Hume, *Dialogues Concerning Natural Religion*

Cleanthes* provides the opposing view, that of anthropomorphism, according to which God has person-like qualities, and in particular, a psychology (a mental character useful in our understanding of his behavior). God *loves* humankind (so has emotions), God *knows* everything (so has beliefs), God *wants* humankind to be good (so has desires), and so on. God is a *super*-person, of course, but similar in many respects to a human person.

Cleanthes starts with the argument from design.* He holds that if God is the world's designer and we can appreciate his handiwork by observing the world, then that sheds some light on the nature of the designer.

Philo* introduces the opposing argument: the "argument from evil."*[2] He suggests that the existence of evil is incompatible with the existence of a theistic* God who intervenes directly in human affairs. There are different ways of using this argument, but perhaps the simplest is this: If God is omnipotent,* omniscient,* and omnibenevolent,* (all-powerful, all-knowing, and all-good), then there should be no evil in the world. But there is evil in the world. So either God does not exist, or he isn't omnipotent, omniscient, or omnibenevolent. By definition, however, God is omnipotent, omniscient, and omnibenevolent—so his existence is impossible.

Exploring the Ideas

When Demea introduces mysticism into the debate, it seems at first as if Philo agrees with him that we cannot know the nature of God. But by "God" Demea means "the original cause of this universe."[3] It is easy to miss the significance of this. If "the cause of the universe" is all the term "God" means, then the claim that God exists becomes fairly insubstantial. This is known as the "emptiness problem" and it is not easy for mysticism to solve.

On the one hand, asserting that God's nature is unknowable seems to lead to the emptiness problem. On the other, trying to avoid the emptiness problem by saying more about what one means by "God" seems to lead directly away from mysticism. That is the mystic's dilemma—embrace emptiness or abandon mysticism.

In *Dialogues*, Cleanthes attacks Demea on this very point.[4] As he states: "*Mystics* ... are, in a word, atheists,* without knowing it. For though it be allowed, that Deity possesses attributes, of which we have no comprehension; yet ought we never to ascribe him any attributes, which are absolutely incompatible with that intelligent nature, essential to him. A mind whose acts and sentiments and ideas are not distinct and successive; one that is wholly simple, and totally immutable; is a mind, which has no thought, no reason, no will, no sentiment, no love, no hatred; or, in a word, is no mind at all."

Such anti-mystical arguments are given a positive hearing in *Dialogues*, and Cleanthes' human-like God seems to have the upper hand for much of the text. Cleanthes faces his own difficulties, though, when Philo puts forward the argument from evil.

Cleanthes struggles in the face of Philo's two-pronged attack. Philo talks about the "consistency problem of evil"*—the argument that the existence of evil is inconsistent with the existence of a theistic God. Philo, however, then presents the "inference problem of evil" and corners natural theologian* Cleanthes using his own empiricist* principles. The inference problem is this: empiricists should form inferences from how the world is; if they wish to infer from the nature of the world the existence of an intelligent designer, then they should infer the nature of that designer from the nature of the world. But considering the world with all its cruelties, the best anyone could say about its designer is that he is indifferent to suffering.

Overlooked

Dialogues has been read closely by many great thinkers since it was published in the late eighteenth century; the text's ingenious subtlety has generated a long and lively debate on the matter of its interpretation. As one of the world's most widely discussed philosophical texts, it is difficult to identify anything that has been overlooked with regard to its philosophical content.

But *Dialogues* is a literary masterpiece as much as a philosophical one; it is perhaps a pity that its status as a philosophical text of great worth has overshadowed is substance as an extraordinary work of literature in a wider sense. It has been left to philosophers to sing the praises of Hume's style, which they have certainly done. But for philosophers, of course, the beauty of an argument is a different thing to the literary worth of the prose in which it is couched. It is something of a shame that Hume's literary achievements, in the sense of his stylistic excellence, remain relatively underappreciated.

NOTES

1   David Hume, *Dialogues Concerning Natural Religion*, ed. Stanley Tweyman (London, Routledge, 1991), *Dialogues*, 107.

2   Hume, *Dialogues*, 169.

3   Hume, *Dialogues*, 108.

4   Hume, *Dialogues*, 123.

MODULE 7
ACHIEVEMENT

KEY POINTS

- Hume was a key thinker in the rise of the empiricist* movement, which is still a strong force in modern philosophy.

- The period of European cultural history known as the Enlightenment* saw a challenge to religious authority in many areas of society and thought; Hume's *Dialogues Concerning Natural Religion* was one of the period's significant texts.

- On account of the subtlety of the work's arguments, scholars have disagreed over Hume's true conclusions; this can be seen as reflecting his lifelong delight in provoking good debate.

Assessing the Argument

The success or failure of any set of philosophical ideas, such as those offered by David Hume in his *Dialogues Concerning Natural Religion*, is difficult to measure. We might begin by considering how *consistent* a philosopher has been and the skill and sophistication of his or her approach. By that measure, Hume scores very highly indeed: his commitment to empiricist principles—his emphasis on founding a reasoned argument on the evidence of his senses—never wavers.

This contrasts rather starkly with his opponents who, as *Dialogues Concerning Natural Religion* reveals, have to contend with a number of inherent contradictions in their position. The way Hume marshals the debate to leave his adversaries with an empty victory shows his great argumentative agility and foresight.

Historical trends that followed Hume's contributions also point to the importance of his thought. Empiricism is the central theme in

> ❝ [God is] a Being, so remote and incomprehensible, who bears much less analogy to any other being in the universe than the sun to a waxen taper, and who discovers himself only by some faint traces or outlines, beyond which we have no authority to ascribe to him any attribute or perfection. ❞
>
> David Hume, *An Enquiry Concerning Human Understanding*

almost all of Hume's writing, and the movement drew strength from the author's contributions to modern philosophy. By the middle of the twentieth century a version known as "logical empiricism"* established itself as the most powerful empiricist movement philosophy has ever seen.[1] Although it eventually faltered (as pretty much all philosophical movements do), it generated more complex empiricist approaches that remain popular today.[2] That popularity is Hume's intellectual legacy. Since the turn of the twenty-first century there have been more than 700 articles published with the adjective "Humean" in the title or abstract (an abstract is a brief summary of the content of a longer piece).

If Hume wanted to fuel anti-clerical social forces and skepticism* about God, then there is evidence he was successful. Nearly three quarters of academic philosophers now describe themselves as atheists.[3] And in Hume's native Scotland almost half the population claims to have "no religion."[4] This must have seemed a very distant prospect when Hume was preparing for the controversial *Dialogues* to be published only after he was dead.

Achievement in Context

Dialogues emerged during the "golden period of English theology"*[5] ("theology" here referring to scholarly inquiry into religious principles and texts). While Hume was Scottish, he was writing in

English and so was associated with this period. The tide of Enlightenment thinking raised inquiry to new heights in many disciplines. The new school of natural theology,* meanwhile, fueled a boom in scholarly output. The stage was set for reputations to be made.

Hume's audience would have been formed both of those sympathetic to the work's ideas and those opposed to them. However, he was so worried about how some religious people would react to his arguments that he delayed its publication. While Hume had friends among the more progressive clergy, he had many powerful enemies among more conservative churchmen. At one stage they tried to have him excommunicated—expelled—from the Church of Scotland* (a process tantamount, it was believed, to consigning him to Hell). Hume joked about it in a letter to his friend, the Scottish painter Allan Ramsay:* "You may tell the reverend gentleman the Pope, that there are many here who rail at him, and yet would be much greater persecutors had they equal power. The last Assembly sat on me. They did not propose to burn me, because they cannot. But they intend to give me over to Satan, which they think they have the power of doing. My friends, however, prevailed, and my damnation is postponed for a twelvemonth."[6]

Despite all this, *Dialogues* was no *succès de scandale*—a work that finds success simply by being controversial. It caused few ripples in public life when it was eventually published. Yet the work had wide-ranging effects, as it was read and built upon by many of Europe's leading thinkers in the years that followed.

Limitations

Subtlety is both the text's main strength and its chief weakness. While scholars have been analyzing it for more than two centuries, and much valuable work has been generated by the detailed and lengthy debates over how to interpret Hume's writing, this has perhaps undermined the book's effectiveness. If one accepts the standard reading of *Dialogues* as being skeptical toward the existence of God, then the fact that a significant number of commentators have argued that the book should be read as *supporting* belief in God[7] should give us cause to reflect on the nature of its success.

Hume never lived to see such disagreements over his views, so was unable settle the argument by spelling out his conclusions more clearly. If he had been alive to do so, he may have been at pains to make his philosophical points in other ways for the elimination of doubt. Judging by his body of work, Hume rarely backed down from an argument and was more than willing to engage with his adversaries. So it is easy to imagine Hume enjoying the fact that the variety of interpretations demonstrates that there is a good deal of truth in his claim that nothing could have been "more cautiously and more artfully written."[8]

NOTES

1   See Stephen P. Schwartz, *A Brief History of Analytic Philosophy* (London: Wiley-Blackwell, 2012), 46–101.

2   See Schwartz, *A Brief History*, 76–118; see also David Bourget and David J. Chalmers, "What Do Philosophers Believe?" *Philosophical Studies* 170 (2014): 465–500.

3   See Bourget and Chalmers, "What Do Philosophers Believe?," 490.

4   Scottish Television News, "Almost Half of Scots Not Religious, According to New Figures," August 26, 2015, http://news.stv.tv/scotland/1327477-almost-half-of-scots-not-religious-according-to-scottish-household-survey/.

5   Paul Russell, "Hume on Religion," in *The Stanford Encyclopedia of Philosophy,* ed. Edward N. Zalta (Stanford: Metaphysics *Research Lab CSLI,* 2014), http://plato.stanford.edu/archives/win2014/entries/hume-religion/, §1.

6   David Hume, "To Allan Ramsay," in *The Letters of David Hume*, vol. I, ed. J.

Y. T. Greig (Oxford: Clarendon Press, 1932), 224.

7   See Ronald J. Butler, "Natural Belief and the Enigma of Hume," *Archiv für die Geschichte der Philosophie* 42 (1960): 73–100. See also Stanley Tweyman, *Scepticism and Belief in Hume's Dialogues Concerning Natural Religion* (Dordrecht: Kluwer, 1981), 121–56.

8   David Hume, "To Adam Smith," in *The Letters of David Hume*, vol. II, ed. J. Y. T. Greig (Oxford: Clarendon Press, 1932), 334.

MODULE 8
PLACE IN THE AUTHOR'S WORK

KEY POINTS

- Hume's main philosophical mission in *Dialogues Concerning Natural Religion* is to defend and develop empiricism,* the school of thought that holds that knowledge stems only from sensory information.

- The work offers a demonstration of Hume's skeptical* thinking, challenging anything he considered dogma (that is, orthodox, unquestioned belief) or superstition, and questioning the very nature of reality.

- Many scholars consider *Dialogues*, Hume's final published work, to be his finest; the debate is complicated by the extraordinary quality of his other writing.

Positioning

The theme connecting *Dialogues Concerning Natural Religion* to David Hume's other philosophical work is that of empiricism. The idea that sensory experience is the source of all knowledge runs through Hume's writing from his first thoughts as a young man to his posthumous publication of *Dialogues*. In the first of his major works, *A Treatise of Human Nature*, for example, Hume suggested that all of philosophy and science should be based on empirical investigation.

Hume developed a wide-ranging and sophisticated empiricist philosophical system throughout his life as a writer. *A Treatise of Human Nature* was published in parts between 1739 and 1740 and laid down the foundation of Hume's empiricism. He extended and developed his philosophy in a number of other works, including *Enquiry Concerning Human Understanding* (1748), *An Enquiry Concerning the Principles of Morals* (1751), *Essays and Treatises on Several Subjects* (1754), and *Four Dissertations* (1757).

> ❝ Some years ago, I composed a piece, which would make a small Volume in Twelves. I call it *Dialogues on natural religion*. Some of my friends flatter me, that it is the best thing I ever wrote. ❞
>
> David Hume, *The Letters of David Hume*, vol. II

Dialogues appeared in 1779, three years after his death, and was his last published work. The book brings together Hume's thoughts on a key consequence of his commitment to empiricism—that it leaves little room for religious belief. Although Hume published some of his thoughts on religion in previous works, such as a discussion of miracles in *An Enquiry Concerning the Principles of Morals*, *Dialogues* is his most thorough examination of belief in God. For this reason, *Dialogues* occupies an important position in his life's work. The book contains his final thoughts on the implications that empiricism holds for religious belief.

Integration

The fashion among scholars in Hume's era was to produce grand philosophical systems. A single approach was used to address all the problems of philosophy. Hume was no exception, and he tried to integrate all of the philosophical problems he addressed into his empiricist world view.

Hume's empiricism was also skeptical in character. He quickly dismissed what he saw as dogma or superstition if it was not supported empirically. This included religious beliefs, but it also included features of reality considered essential components of ontology* (the study of what exists).

One famous example is Hume's supposed skepticism* about causation.[1] While this reading is controversial, some argue it is a consequence of his firm-footed empiricism.[2] If all we can rely on for knowledge is sensory experience, and if this experience provides evidence that events follow each other in regular ways, then all we have learned is that events are regular in a specific way. We have not found evidence that any event *causes* another.

A car's shadow is cast on the road. A moment later, the car's shadow is cast on another part of the road. But no one would conclude that the first shadow caused the second shadow; the event of the car being struck by sunlight from a certain angle caused both shadows.

One event following another is not enough to show any cause or causes—but sensory experience presents us with a succession of events. We experience only the "shadows" and are not justified in claiming we can know anything else.

Hume's position with regard to the very existence of causation has provoked much debate; it is probably enough here to acknowledge that the existence of this debate serves to remind us of both his skepticism and his commitment to empiricist thought. Skeptical empiricism is woven through *Dialogues* and fits Hume's wider philosophy.

Significance

While there is no consensus on which of Hume's works is the greatest, it is widely agreed that *Dialogues* ranks among his best.[3] The lack of a unanimous decision does not come from wildly differing views over the quality of *Dialogues*. The book is widely regarded as a philosophical and literary masterpiece—but then so are all his others.

Some scholars are convinced that *Dialogues* is superior to Hume's other work, however. His contemporary Edward Gibbon,* one of the greatest historians of the modern period, held that the book was "the most profound, the most ingenious, and the best written."[4] It is not difficult to see why. The book is unique in Hume's output as the only dialogue, and it contains some of his most mature and carefully constructed work.

The book was long in the making: while the first draft was completed in 1751, the text in its final published form was completed in 1776 (partly on account of Hume's hesitance in publishing before his death).

It is also arguably his most *intriguing* work, full of sleights of hand, deft touches, puzzles, and problems to ponder, all contained within that most enigmatic of philosophical forms: the dialogue. This explains the nature of the work's appeal; we may expect the text's status as something of an unsolved mystery to continue to attract the attention of the philosophically curious.

NOTES

1 See William Edward Morris and Charlotte R. Brown, "David Hume," in *The Stanford Encyclopedia of Philosophy*, ed. Edward N. Zalta (Stanford: Metaphysics *Research Lab CSLI,* 2014), http://plato.stanford.edu/archives/sum2014/entries/hume/, 5.

2 Morris and Brown, "David Hume," 5.

3 William Lad Sessions, *Reading Hume's Dialogues: A Veneration for True Religion* (Bloomington: Indiana University Press, 2002), 1.

4 Quoted in Dorothy Coleman (Ed.), "Introduction," in *Hume: Dialogues Concerning Natural Religion and Other Writings* (Cambridge: Cambridge University Press, 2007), xi.

SECTION 3
IMPACT

MODULE 9
THE FIRST RESPONSES

KEY POINTS

- Most early critics thought *Dialogues* showed Hume to be an atheist* and argued that the character Philo* was his mouthpiece.

- By the middle of the nineteenth century, Hume was increasingly difficult to ignore, with the evolutionary theory* proposed by the English naturalist Charles Darwin* offering an explanation for the appearance of "design" in nature in which God was not necessary.

- The fiercest criticism of Hume's ideas came from dominant conservative religious forces in society.

Criticism

The word that most commonly greeted David Hume's *Dialogues Concerning Natural Religion* was "atheist." Many took the character Philo to be Hume's mouthpiece for atheist argument,[1] despite Philo and Cleanthes* apparently agreeing by the end of the book that God exists. This ending has sparked huge debate. One theory is that Philo's apparent U-turn is an empty concession. Philo takes "God" as merely the uncaused cause of the universe about which we can know virtually nothing, so this counts for very little.

Critics in the late 1700s were not as sold on this interpretation as later scholars have been. The perception among believers that Hume was an atheist drove much of the first response to *Dialogues*. There was widespread cynicism regarding his motives and outrage at his challenge to cherished beliefs. The religious scholar Thomas Hayter* wrote the first sustained attack on *Dialogues*, asking, "Has skeptical* philosophy

❝ The fact indeed indisputably is, that Philo, not Cleanthes, personates Mr Hume. ❞

Thomas Hayter, *Remarks on Mr. Hume's Dialogues*

any balm to comfort the devout heart; any medicine to refresh the religiously-afflicted spirit? Let us, in imagination, consign the religionist to Philo's direction, and watch the result."[2]

Many were convinced that Philo was both an atheist and the victor of *Dialogues*. The English theologian Joseph Priestley,* who was also an expert in a number of other subjects, declared that "though the debate seemingly closes on the side of the theist,* the victory is clearly on the side of the atheist."[3] Such responses set the tone, remaining the standard view for decades after *Dialogues* was published.

It fell to the influential German philosopher Immanuel Kant* to provide immediate support. He was the most significant scholar to consider Hume's arguments when they first appeared. In his *Critique of Pure Reason* in 1781—five years after the publication of *Dialogues*—Kant agrees with Hume that the argument for a designer of the universe is not sound. He does so, however, with a sense of regret.[4]

The English philosopher William Paley's* *Natural Theology* (1802) grappled with many of the issues in *Dialogues*, but he chose not to criticize Hume directly. Instead he shadow-boxed Hume by constructing responses without mentioning him explicitly. Paley's text had an immense reputation for much of the nineteenth century and contains the definitive expression of the argument from design.*[5]

It is telling that Paley's veiled attempts to beat Hume's arguments were popular but not well reasoned. They often relied on little more than bold assertion. The dogmatic criticism that Hume tried so hard to avoid in his artful construction of *Dialogues* remained alive and well.

Responses

It was not until the nineteenth century that Hume's arguments began to be given the hearing they deserved. The publication of the English naturalist Charles Darwin's* *On the Origin of Species* (1859), in which he elaborated the principles of evolutionary theory,* provoked a revolution in Western thought. Darwin's text struck a decisive blow in favor of the empiricist* critique of the argument from design. A mechanism to explain the appearance of design in nature had been found, and the argument that the universe must have had a designer because it appeared to have been designed could no longer be supported.

In many respects, Darwin finished the work that Hume started. The argument from design had long been the position of choice for intellectually respectable religious scholars and was almost universally accepted in nineteenth-century polite society.[6] But after Darwin, the tide turned.

Darwin's great idea was as simple to digest as it was radical. Natural selection is a mechanism whereby the population of any given species evolves over time. Any organism that is best suited to its environment has an increased chance of survival and, therefore, an increased chance of producing offspring. These offspring are also better suited to the environmental conditions and the cycle is repeated over and over until nature has weeded out those less suited to the environment. The species, in other words, has evolved.

Later advances in knowledge about the precise biological mechanisms at work in the process of evolution have not changed the implications of Darwin's insights. In this beautiful explanation he successfully challenged the best examples used by defenders of the design argument. A divine designer was no longer required to explain the appearance of design.

Conflict and Consensus

Darwin's theory of evolution had not only formed the basis of any challenge to the concept of a designed world, it had another striking implication as well: every living thing on Earth was probably descended from a common ancestor.

This had devastating implications for the religion of the day. Darwin's scientific theory of evolution threatened to defeat natural theology*—the rational justification of religious claims. The matter was contentious. Prominent churchmen brought their most fervent rhetoric to bear in a series of public disputes. Initially, religious objections took second place to objections from the scientific community. Darwin's most vociferous opponents, however, usually consisted of those who bridged both the religious and the scientific worlds, such as the biologist St. George Jackson Mivart.* Attempts by people like Mivart to reconcile Darwin's theory with religious belief steadily lost ground as Darwin's ideas began to be supported by an unassailable body of evidence.

The contest was fierce, however, with religious voices raised as they had been against Hume. In 1860, a debate was held on Darwin's ideas at the British Association for the Advancement of Science in Oxford. In the anti-Darwin corner was Bishop Samuel Wilberforce,* an uncompromising debater. In the pro-Darwin corner was Professor Thomas Huxley,* later known as "Darwin's bulldog."

Wilberforce tried to ridicule the "insulting" notion that people were merely "improved apes" rather than God's "crown and perfection."[7] He asked if Huxley was descended from apes on his grandmother's or grandfather's side,[8] at which point Huxley said to a colleague, "The Lord hath delivered him into mine hands,"[9] before replying to Wilberforce that he "would rather be descended from an ape than from a man who used his intellect and influence to introduce ridicule into a grave scientific discussion."[10]

NOTES

1   See James Fieser, *Early Responses to Hume's Life and Reputation*, vols 9 and 10 (London: Bloomsbury, 2003).

2   Quoted in Tweyman, *Hume on Natural Religion*, 78.

3   Quoted in Martin Priestman, *Romantic Atheism: Poetry and Freethought, 1780–1830* (Cambridge: Cambridge University Press, 2007), 18.

4   See Immanuel Kant, *Critique of Pure Reason*, trans. N. Kemp Smith (London: Macmillan, 1976), 518–24.

5   See William Paley, *Natural Theology: Or Evidences of the Existence and Attributes of the Deity Collected from the Appearances of Nature* (Boston: Gould and Lincoln, 1867), 1.

6   Andrew Pyle, *Hume's Dialogues Concerning Natural Religion* (London: Continuum, 2006), 138–9.

7   Thomas Dixon, *Science and Religion: A Very Short Introduction* (Oxford: Oxford University Press, 2008), 74.

8   Dixon, *Science and Religion*, 74.

9   Dixon, *Science and Religion*, 74.

10 Dixon, *Science and Religion*, 74.

MODULE 10
THE EVOLVING DEBATE

KEY POINTS

- Hume's influence continued to grow in the nineteenth and twentieth centuries as new schools of empiricism* flourished.

- Logical empiricism* enjoyed a mid-twentieth-century heyday when thinkers used highly technical, sophisticated arguments to counter the rationalist* questions Hume himself had faced.

- Though Western interest in the philosophy of religion has waned, empiricism is still going strong and *Dialogues* makes a contribution to modern debates.

Uses and Problems

Debates about religious belief have continued to evolve since the publication of David Hume's *Dialogues Concerning Natural Religion* and his influence has varied depending on the philosophical fashions of the day.

One famous commentator was the major Victorian intellectual John Stuart Mill.* Although he was an empiricist like Hume, Mill thought the argument from design* was the best defense of natural theology.* He was unconvinced by Darwin's theory of evolution. In Mill's words, "Leaving aside [the theory of evolution] to whatever fate the progress of discovery may have in store for it, I think it must be allowed that … the adaptations in nature afford a large balance of probability in favor of creation by intelligence. It is equally certain that this is no more than a probability."[1]

❝ What a book a Devil's chaplain might write, on the clumsy, wasteful, blundering low and horridly cruel works of nature! ❞
Charles Darwin, in a letter to his friend Joseph Hooker

Mill used this to defend a position between theism* (the belief that God is all-powerful and intervenes directly in human affairs) and deism* (the belief that God is the architect of the universe, but that it runs itself perfectly in his absence). This position was that God, although not quite the absent figure of deism, was limited in his power and perfections.[2]

After Mill the twentieth century dawned, ushering in a new generation of philosophers who shared Hume's conviction that knowledge could only come from sensory experience, not from pure abstract reasoning. Theirs was a very self-confident variety of empiricism.

Schools of Thought

Twentieth-century philosophers such as Moritz Schlick* of Germany and the British thinker A. J. Ayer* began an attempt to combine the ideas of empiricism with the system of mathematical logic* associated with the German mathematician Gottlob Frege* and the Anglo Austrian philosopher Ludwig Wittgenstein.* The result is what became known as "logical empiricism" (also known as "neo-positivism").* Rationalists had pointed to mathematics in an attempt to argue that not *all* knowledge had to come by means of sensory experience, as the empiricists had it. The neo-positivists, encouraged by the works of the British philosopher Bertrand Russell,* were able to draw attention to a verification principle* whereby they argued that any concept that was not verifiable was devoid of meaning.[3]

This was combined with the idea that all logical truths are *tautologies* (or, more exactly, tautologies are compounds that come out true regardless of what propositions they are composed of). One well-known tautology is "P or not P." We can substitute any statement for "P" ("I live on Mars" or "Grass is always pink" will do) and "P or not P" will always be true: "I live on Mars or it is not the case that I live on Mars" must be true. Likewise, "Grass is always pink or it's not the case that grass is always pink" must be true.

Mathematical truths are logical so they cannot be untrue; they are only true if they are true. We can also find linguistic tautologies; these are statements that cannot be untrue for the same reason.

In mathematics, then, knowledge takes precedence over experience; a priori* reasoning can bring us to knowledge.

These tautologies, however, do not purport to describe the world; they are not *analytic*, that is, being only self-referential and self-affirming truths. In this, they offer no counter argument to the empiricist argument that all knowledge is gathered by means of the senses.[3]

This "logical empiricist" proposal was a highly technical, sophisticated expression of Humean empiricism in its most far-reaching form. Logical empiricists, like Hume before them, tried to "commit metaphysics* to the flames," along with nearly all of traditional philosophy ("metaphysics" here being used in the sense of the reasoned exploration of reality, including such areas that are the province of religious thought). The logical empiricists did this by adopting a strong (very Humean) empiricist theory of meaning. Only those propositions that were empirically verifiable, or tautologies, were meaningful. Against such a position, most of the claims of traditional philosophy, never mind religion, were under threat. This was the empiricist project at its peak.[4]

In Current Scholarship

Modern philosophers of religion still grapple with the issue that preoccupies Hume in *Dialogues*—understanding belief in God. The big question is whether the rules of evidentialism* apply. Evidentialism is the position that a belief can only be justified if it is backed by enough evidence. Many accept that religious beliefs fail this kind of measure. They are not self-evident or conclusively supported by other evidence. Hume and his followers, then, have largely won that debate.

For some scholars, however, evidentialism does not apply to religious belief. The US philosopher Alvin Plantinga's* defense of reformed epistemology,* for example, which sets out to give an account of how religious beliefs might be "warranted" despite not being justified in the evidentialist sense, is an example.[5]

If philosophy of religion has declined as a central concern for Western thinkers, this is partly because social changes have seen religion decline in significance in many cultures. What is more, the current fashion in philosophy is to be scientific. Precision and clarity are increasingly valued alongside technical work that uses formal languages like logic* and mathematics. In fact contemporary philosophy is sometimes criticized for its excessively dry and technical character (or contemporary philosophy of the dominant variety, at least).[6]

Empiricism, however, remains in vogue, as does work on broadly Humean themes in metaphysics and epistemology* (the study of the nature, limits, and so on, of knowledge), which forms a central part of much cutting-edge work today.[7] In this way, Hume still makes a major contribution to the contemporary debate.

NOTES

1   John Stuart Mill, *Three Essays on Religion* (Bristol: Thoemmes Press, 1993), 176–95.

2   Mill, *Three Essays*, 176–95.

3   Stephen P. Schwartz, *A Brief History of Analytic Philosophy* (London: Wiley-Blackwell, 2012), 50–62.

4   Schwartz, *A Brief History of Analytic Philosophy*, 64–70.

5   Peter Forrest, "The Epistemology of Religion," in *The Stanford Encyclopedia of Philosophy, ed.* Edward N. Zalta (Stanford: Metaphysics *Research Lab CSLI,* 2014), http://plato.stanford.edu/archives/spr2014/entries/religion-epistemology/, esp. § 7.

6   See Hans-Johann Glock, *What is Analytic Philosophy?* (Cambridge: Cambridge University Press, 2008), 1–4.

7   This was ascertained by using *philpapers.org* to do an "advanced" search for all papers with the phrase "Humean" and "metaphysics" or "epistemology" in the title or abstract since the year 2000.

MODULE 11
IMPACT AND INFLUENCE TODAY

KEY POINTS

- *Dialogues* laid the intellectual groundwork for major discoveries that shaped the modern world; it still fuels efforts to get to grips with the nature of reality and knowledge.

- Twenty-first-century thinkers responding to Hume's text include those who continue to search for ways to strengthen the defense of religious belief in the face of the arguments he makes in *Dialogues*.

- One area of debate is around the idea of whether the way nature appears to be "fine-tuned" helps the case of believers in God—or believers in Hume.

Position

David Hume's *Dialogues Concerning Natural Religion* serves many purposes today. It stands as a *tour de force* of philosophical argument and a work of enormous literary significance. It contains distinguished ideas still debated in one form or another in the twenty-first century. This is all testament to Hume's genius and proof of his being ahead of his time.

Dialogues is an extraordinarily influential work that we can expect to endure as a classic reflection on human attempts to justify belief in God. The debates it provoked in the period after its publication laid the intellectual groundwork for major discoveries that shaped the modern world. These include the evolutionary theory* of Charles Darwin* and the rise of empirical methods in how we seek and gather knowledge. Hume's empiricist principles in *Dialogues* remain of central interest to philosophers working in the vanguard of modern

> ❝ The *Dialogues* are currently recognized as both a
> literary and a philosophical masterpiece—some Hume
> scholars even suggest that they are his finest work. They
> are praised both for the wit and style of the writing and
> for their serious philosophical message, which is, in a
> single word, *empiricism*.* ❞
>
> Andrew Pyle, *Hume's Dialogues Concerning Natural Religion*

scholarship. The more radical ideas of logical positivism (an approach in the field of philosophy according to which, roughly, if a philosophical problem cannot be solved logically then it was not a meaningful problem in the first place) have come under attack in the years following the late 1940s. But empiricism itself has achieved an all-but-total victory over mysticism* through the adoption of fundamentally empirical scientific principles of research and analysis throughout the academic world.

It has been suggested that if we are to sum up Hume's legacy in a single word, it would be "empiricism." *Dialogues* is the finest example of Hume's commitment to the doctrine and the advancements it has afforded us.

Interaction
Modern defenders of a belief in God and others who reject Hume's views on religion have moved the debate on in important ways. Philosophers of religion such as Alvin Plantinga* have produced sophisticated explorations of human knowledge in order to respond to critiques such as Hume's.

A current hot topic that Hume deals with in *Dialogues* is how we understand religious beliefs. One popular response to objections to the theistic* position (that is, the position of those who claim that there is a God who intervenes in human affairs) is to move the debate beyond the language of natural theology* and back to questions about the rationality of faith and other forms of belief not directly supported by rational argument.

Another lively debate in philosophy of religion concerns reformed epistemology*—an attempt to understand the circumstances under which religious beliefs are "warranted" even if they are not, as Hume would have understood it, justified.[1] In exploring such approaches, theists* appear to be tacitly admitting that the old concerns of revealed theologians* (religious scholars who put store in scripture recording divine revelations) were justified—that it was not a particularly good move for theists to try to engage in debates in which reason played an important role. It remains to be seen how successful this work will be.[2]

The Continuing Debate

More straightforward attempts to counter Hume's arguments include defending the idea of a God-designed world by pointing to the "fine-tuning" that appears in the laws of nature. If gravity, for example, were slightly stronger or slightly weaker there could be no stars, planets, or life. And many laws of nature seem to be "just right" in this way.

Those who make this argument then resort to a classic move: they challenge their opponent to come up with a "natural" explanation for this fine-tuning. Then, in the absence of a plausible answer, they might say that a divine designer is the best explanation. This is countered by some variation of the anthropic principle:* we should not be surprised that the universe is conducive to life, since if it were not, we would not be around to question its nature.

While there is something to be said for this line of thought, the arguments Hume makes in *Dialogues* still have relevance here. Why infer a designer from what appears to have been designed when infinite time and chance can do the rest? With infinite time anything can occur, including our universe.

When assessing the complex debate concerning the existence of God, it is important to look at the whole picture. The cut and thrust of a single argument is not enough to settle the issue. *Dialogues* itself is a shining example of the need to see the wider debate play out.

NOTES

1   See Peter Forrest, "The Epistemology of Religion," in *The Stanford Encyclopedia of Philosophy, ed.* Edward N. Zalta (Stanford: Metaphysics *Research Lab CSLI,* 2014), http://plato.stanford.edu/archives/spr2014/ entries/religion-epistemology/, 7.

2   See Forrest, "The Epistemology of Religion."

MODULE 12
WHERE NEXT?

KEY POINTS

- *Dialogues* remains a classic text; its arguments are still to be bested.

- Hume's empiricist* philosophy is still relevant in the continuing battles concerning scientific and religious interpretations of the nature of humanity and the cosmos.

- More than 200 years after it was published, *Dialogues* is considered by many scholars and thinkers to be the best work of the greatest philosopher the English-speaking world has produced.

Potential

The position of David Hume's *Dialogues Concerning Natural Religion* among the best-known and most authoritative texts in philosophy of religion in particular, and in philosophy in general, seems secure. More than 200 years have passed since its publication, yet no one has proposed arguments to decisively counter those Hume makes in it. The influence and relevance the work has had are deserved on the grounds of its ideas. Or, more precisely, many of the *Dialogues'* arguments still stand in their essential form. The debate has of course moved on significantly since Hume's time.

The ball, then, is in the court of those who wish to knock Hume's arguments down. There is ongoing work in philosophy of religion toward that end, but it must be noted that the opinion of the wider philosophical community is that Hume was essentially correct in his central contentions.[1] It is unusual for philosophers to reach a consensus or even a majority opinion on any matter of philosophical interest. So

> **❝ The human being is justified, as rational, in testing all claims, all doctrines which impose respect upon him, before he submits to them. ❞**
> Immanuel Kant,* *Religion within the Bounds of Mere Reason*

the degree of agreement regarding the essentials of Hume's conclusion is striking. Nearly three quarters of contemporary philosophers identify as atheists.*[2] There is no other major position in contemporary philosophy that produces such widespread agreement.[3] In short, defenders of belief in God appear to be losing the argument, just as they do in *Dialogues*.

Future Directions

Philosophy of religion may no longer be such a central concern for as many scholars, but the most promising lines of inquiry are definitely those that bear the name "Humean" in contemporary metaphysics* and epistemology.* Modern views that take Hume's name are strongly empiricist in character and highly suspicious of obscure metaphysical assertions such as those increasingly found in contemporary philosophy since the resurgence in metaphysics that began in the 1970s.[4]

One Humean puzzle is whether things that exist in time and space are connected to one another. This question can be found everywhere in classical metaphysics in one form or another. God necessarily being the cause of the universe is one aspect of this, but there are many others. Claims of "necessary connections" have been put to many uses in contemporary metaphysics (as a means to describe the relationship between mind and body, for example). But Humeans are suspicious of such ideas. Taking their lead from Hume, for whom "necessity" was a relation that held only between ideas in our minds, they hold that these necessary connections lack proper empirical support. This debate is not likely to be resolved easily or quickly.

Further strides are being made in developing naturalistic explanations of widespread religious belief. The American philosopher Daniel Dennett* suggests that religious belief comes from a kind of evolutionary process acting on ideas (as opposed to coming from genes).[5] Dennett belongs to a group sometimes known as the "new atheists"—a loose connection of assertive atheists who put forward confident criticisms of religious belief and its influence on society.[6]

Summary

The status of *Dialogues* as one of the great classics of Western philosophy is reason enough to read it. The book lays out central arguments around God's existence and the opposition between revealed theology* and natural theology;* these matters continue to inform philosophical debates in various ways.

Hume was ahead of his time with the contributions he made to the debate on God's existence and how that existence should be justified. His impact on the overall discussion, in which he unpicked orthodox belief in God through extraordinarily subtle and sophisticated means, has never been equaled. Hume's criticism of the argument from design* and the cosmological argument* are even considered by some to adequately prove such claims for the existence of God to be false.[7]

Dialogues is a perfect example of the Enlightenment* ideal of civil rational inquiry into even the thorniest of subjects. Hume takes on no less a subject than the existence of God and marshals the debate to a standard only a philosopher of his stature could achieve. Many consider him to be the greatest philosopher to have written in English; most consider *Dialogues* to be his finest work. If they are correct, then *Dialogues* endures as the greatest philosophical work ever written in English.

NOTES

1   David Bourget and David J. Chalmers, "What Do Philosophers Believe?" from *Philosophical Studies* 170 (2014): 470.

2   Bourget and Chalmers, "What Do Philosophers Believe?" 465–500.

3   Bourget and Chalmers "What Do Philosophers Believe?" 465–500.

4   See Stephen P. Schwartz, *A Brief History of Analytic Philosophy* (London: Wiley-Blackwell, 2012), 201–38.

5   See Daniel Dennett, *Breaking the Spell: Religion as a Natural Phenomenon* (London: Penguin, 2006).

6   See James E. Taylor, "The New Atheists," in *The Internet Encyclopedia of Philosophy*, ed. J. Fieser and B. Dowden (2015), http://www.iep.utm.edu/n-atheis/.

7   See Simon Blackburn, interview by Nigel Warburton, *fivebooks.com*, July 8, 2013, http://fivebooks.com/interviews/simon-blackburn-on-david-hume.

GLOSSARY

GLOSSARY OF TERMS

A priori: a belief based on theoretical deduction rather than empirical observation.

Agnostic: an adherent of agnosticism (the view that one cannot know whether God does, or does not, exist).

Agnosticism: the view that one cannot know whether God does, or does not, exist.

Anthropic principle: this principle explains how the fact that the universe contains all the necessary elements necessary for human existence is not evidence of a designer since, if the universe were built any other way, we would not exist and therefore would be unable to question its nature.

Argument from design: an argument used in defense of the existence of God, according to which the universe appears designed, and if it appears designed, then the universe must be so; if the universe is designed, then the universe had a designer. If the universe had a designer, then that designer is God. Thus, there is a God.

Argument from evil: an argument used against the existence of God. If God is omnipotent, the argument goes, he can eliminate evil wherever he finds it. If God is omniscient, then he knows where all evil is. If God is omnibenevolent, then he desires to eliminate all evil. Thus, if God exists, there can be no evil in the world. But there is—so God does not exist.

Atheism: the view that God does not exist.

Atheist: an adherent of atheism.

British empiricism: a powerful philosophical school that arose in Britain during the Enlightenment. The school held that the source of knowledge is sensory experience, and denied such things as the existence of innate ideas.

Calvinist: an adherent or example of Calvinism, a major variant of the Protestant faith characterized by an austere form of worship that rejects the typical adornments and accompaniments of Roman Catholic worship. To describe someone as "Calvinist" is often taken to imply that she or he is severe, rigid, and lacking in color and humor.

Church of Scotland: the established Church in Scotland, which is Protestant and Presbyterian.

Cosmological argument: an argument made in defense of the existence of God according to which the universe has a cause and that cause cannot be contingent (that is, dependent on something else for its existence); if that cause cannot be contingent then it must be necessary. The only necessary entity is God—so God exists.

Deism: Deists view God as the architect of the universe. According to deism, God is the creator of the universe, but it runs itself perfectly in His absence, and He does not interfere in that universe, including in the events of human history. Deism was perhaps the most intellectually respectable theological position for scholars to take in the Enlightenment period. There has been some debate about the compatibility of deism and Christianity.

Dialogue: a kind of play in which different characters debate with each other. Many works of philosophy, particularly ancient works, are written as dialogues.

Empiricism: the view that the ultimate source of all knowledge is sensory experience. As a theory of meaning, "empiricism," in its simplest form, is the view that a statement is meaningful if, and only if, it is a statement that reports a sensory experience, or an idea built out of sensory experiences.

Enlightenment: Sometimes known as the "Age of Reason," the Enlightenment (roughly the period from the early seventeenth century to the late eighteenth century) is often characterized as a time when rational inquiry came to dominate the workings of European societies, overthrowing superstition and religious belief.

Epistemology: the study of the nature, limits, source, and structure of knowledge.

Evidentialism: a logical justification that dictates that any conclusion can only be justified by the evidence used to reach said conclusion.

Evolutionary theory: the theoretical understanding of the principles by which organisms, descended from a common ancestor, pass on characteristics to their descendants, and by which species and behavior are formed.

Fideism: the view that to demand reason in support of a religious belief held on the basis of faith—a special kind of believing maintained in the absence of reason—is simply to demand something irrelevant.

Intelligent design: the idea that the complexity and apparent perfection of the constitution of plants and animals somehow proves the existence of a divine "designer."

Intelligentsia: the class of individuals in a society who, through their mental labor, shape that society. In modern societies, the intelligentsia is largely made up of academics, politicians, journalists, some business figures, and other educated members of society who contribute to the debates of the day.

Logic: the study of reason. A logic is a codification of rules of inference and truth conditions for a language.

Logical empiricism: also known as logical positivism, this is a philosophical movement that began in the 1920s. Its core argument was that only statements that could be verified via either logic or empirical research had any real meaning.

Mathematical logic: a branch of mathematics that investigates the application of logic to mathematics.

Metaphysics: the study of the ultimate features of reality, such as time, space, events, objects, properties, relations, and modality.

Mysticism: this seeks to find harmony with the transcendental, which Kant defined as anything that it was impossible to know or understand. So, even though God is unknowable and proof of his existence cannot be verified, supporters of mysticism believe we can still learn something of the world via the mechanisms of things such as prayer or contemplation. The word also refers generally to ill-defined spiritual belief.

Natural religion: the doctrine that theological claims should be justified by rational argument as opposed to an appeal to authority.

Natural theology: an important subject in Hume's *Dialogues*, natural theology is an approach used by supporters of natural religion—the doctrine that theological claims should be justified by rational argument as opposed to an appeal to authority. Natural theology is to be distinguished from "revealed theology," which endeavors to justify theological claims by appeal to authority, in the form of either special experiences (revelations) or texts.

Neo Positivism: a twentieth-century branch of sociology that attempted to resolve some of the methodological problems that were challenging philosophy by bridging the gulf between materialism and idealism.

Omnibenevolent: perfectly good. A body with no moral failings.

Omnipotent: all powerful.

Omniscient: all knowing.

Ontology: the study of what exists.

Problem of evil: an argument used against the existence of God. If God is omnipotent, the argument goes, he can eliminate evil wherever he finds it. If God is omniscient, then he knows where all evil is. If God is omnibenevolent, then he desires to eliminate all evil. Thus, if God exists, there can be no evil in the world. But there is: so God does not exist.

Protestant: a term originating in the sixteenth century, used to describe formerly Catholic groups that have renounced the authority of the Roman Catholic Church. The Protestant Church is one of the two major branches of the Christian faith (the other being Roman Catholicism).

Rationalism: an approach to philosophical inquiry according to which we gain at least some knowledge independently of sensory experience (in contrast with empiricism); for rationalists, mathematics is a notable example. The debate between empiricists and rationalists is a central philosophical dispute of the modern period.

Reformed epistemology: part of a religious argument set in opposition to the verification principle. It argues that religious belief can be rational regardless of whether there is any evidence or not.

Revealed theology: the attempt to justify theological claims by appeal to authority, in the form of either special experiences (revelations) or texts.

Skeptic: a person who questions the validity of any assertion or belief that is not supported by empirical evidence. In the modern era, skeptics usually question unsubstantiated claims from a variety of sources, including conspiracy theories, mysticism, and religion.

Skepticism: the questioning of any assertion or belief that is not supported by empirical evidence. In the modern era, it usually involves questioning of unsubstantiated claims from a variety of sources, including conspiracy theories, mysticism, and religion.

Socratic method: the process of engaging in logic-governed examination of a particular belief or theory through a process of question and answer. The method is named for its most famous exponent, the Greek philosopher Socrates, who practices the method as a character in the works of Plato. Plato's many works take the form of a dialogue, and Socrates appears frequently therein, critically examining the beliefs of the other characters, asking after the nature of such things as beauty, truth, and justice.

Succès de scandale: French for "success from scandal." Many successes are the result of scandal, particularly when it comes to selling things, as scandal attracts attention. Hence the phrase "there is no such thing as bad publicity."

Teleological argument: often referred to as the design argument, it stipulates that since the universe appears to have been deliberately designed, its very existence should be taken as evidence for God.

Theism: Theists believe that God is the omnipotent, omniscient, omnibenevolent eternal creator or sustainer of the universe, who intervenes directly in human affairs.

Theist: an adherent of theism. One who believes that God is the omnipotent, omniscient, omnibenevolent eternal creator or sustainer of the universe, who intervenes directly in human affairs.

Theology: the systematic study of religious thought through religious texts; the term also signifies a system of religious belief.

Verification principle: a core statement of the branch of philosophy known as logical positivism. The principle attests that only statements that could be verified logically or empirically had any real meaning.

PEOPLE MENTIONED IN THE TEXT

A. J. Ayer (1910–1989) was a philosopher associated with the field of logical positivism. He was the Wykeham Professor of Logic at Oxford University.

George Berkeley (1685–1753) is best known for his defense of idealism, the thesis that all that exists are minds and the ideas in them. His most famous works are Treatise Concerning the Principles of Human Knowledge (1710) and Three Dialogues between Hylas and Philonous (1713).

Cleanthes is one of the three main characters in the *Dialogues*. In many respects Cleanthes represents liberal theology, defending empiricist natural theology and anthropomorphism about God. Possibly named after Cleanthes of Assos (*c.* 331–232 B.C.E.).

Charles Darwin (1809–82) was a British naturalist and geologist who made revolutionary contributions to biology by proposing the theory of evolution by natural selection. His most famous work is *On the Origin of Species* (1859).

Demea is one of the three main characters in the *Dialogues*. In many respects, Demea represents conservative theology, in particular by defending revealed theology.

Daniel Dennett (b. 1942) is a philosopher and cognitive scientist noted for his work in evolutionary biology and the functioning of the human mind, and the philosophical implications of research in these areas.

Epicurus (341–270 B.C.E.) had a wide-ranging philosophy involving contributions to ethics, empiricist epistemology, and materialism. Sadly, the only written record we have of his views are in three "letters" that he wrote to his followers, reproduced in Diogenes Laertius' Lives of Eminent Philosophers, from the third century B.C.E.

Adam Ferguson (1723–1816) was a moral philosopher and historian often credited with being the father of modern sociology. His most famous work is *An Essay on the History of Civil Society* (1767).

Gottlob Frege (1848–1925) was a German mathematician and logician who is often considered to be one of the founders of the school of analytic philosophy. His best-known work is *Begriffsschrift, eine der arithmetischen nachgebildete Formelsprache des reinen Denkens* (1879).

Edward Gibbon (1737–94) was a famous historian, best known for his great work *The History of the Decline and Fall of the Roman Empire* (1776).

Thomas Hayter (1702–62) was a religious scholar from the English county of Devon. A critic of Hume's work, he served as a bishop for 13 years.

Thomas Hobbes (1588–1679) was a major philosopher in the early modern period. Known today primarily for his contributions to political philosophy, in his day his controversial materialism and atheism were also much discussed. His magnum opus is *Leviathan* (1651).

Francis Hutcheson (1694–1746) is known primarily for his work on moral philosophy and aesthetics. His more notable works include

An Inquiry into the Original of our Ideas of Beauty and Virtue (1725) and A System of Moral Philosophy (1755).

Thomas Henry Huxley (1825–95) was an English biologist and public intellectual perhaps best known for his forceful defense of Darwin's ideas. His most famous work is *Evidence as to Man's place in Nature* (1863).

Immanuel Kant (1724–1804) was a German philosopher of major importance. Kant is considered by some to be the most important philosopher of the modern period. His most famous work is the Critique of Pure Reason (1781).

Leucippus (b. early 400s B.C.E.) was an ancient Greek philosopher noted for his contribution to the theory of atomism—the idea that matter was constructed from indivisible, invisible elements.

John Locke (1632–1704) is often viewed as being the founder of the school of British empiricism. His Essay Concerning Human Understanding (1689) is considered as one of the first, and most significant, defenses of empiricism.

John Stuart Mill (1806–73) was a British philosopher and social theorist noted as a leading figure of the utilitarian approach in moral philosophy, according to which the "best" action is the action that contributes most successfully to human happiness.

St. George Jackson Mivart (1827–1900) was an English biologist and religious scholar noted for his attempts to reconcile Darwinian evolutionary theory with contemporary Catholic theology.

Bishop William Paley (1743–1805) was an English clergyman, Christian apologist, philosopher, and utilitarian. He is best known for his Natural Theology or Evidences of the Existence and Attributes of the Deity, in which he argues for the existence of God by using the analogy of a blind watchmaker—an argument made according to natural theology.

Philo is one of the three main characters of the Dialogues. Philo is the skeptic who many see as the character closest to expressing Hume's views—although whether this is actually the case is controversial. Possibly named after Philo of Larissa (c. 154–84 B.C.E.).

Alvin Plantinga (b. 1932) is an American philosopher best known for his contributions to epistemology and philosophy of religion. His works include God and Other Minds (1967), The Nature of Necessity (1974), and Warranted Christian Belief (2000).

Plato (c. 425–c. 348 B.C.E.) was an ancient Greek philosopher and mathematician. Plato is credited as being one of the founding fathers of Western philosophy and is most famous for his work *The Republic*.

Joseph Priestley (1733–1804) was a scientist, politician, religious scholar, and theologian noted for the invention of soda water, for his identification of several gases, and for his attempts to reconcile Enlightenment rationality with religious thought.

Protagoras (*c.* 490–*c.* 420 B.C.E.) was a Greek philosopher who tackled questions of virtue and politics. Plato labeled him a Sophist, a teacher who taught, among other things, both philosophy and rhetoric.

Allan Ramsay (1713–84) was a famous Scottish painter known for his portraits, and a friend of David Hume.

Thomas Reid (1710–96) made major contributions to epistemology, philosophy of perception, the debate about free will, and philosophical methodology. Reid is a leading figure of the "commonsense" school and his major works include: An Inquiry Into the Human Mind on the Principles of Common Sense (1764) and Essays on the Active Powers of Man (1788).

Bertrand Russell (1872–1970) was a British philosopher who is regarded as one of the founding fathers of the school of analytic philosophy. His Principia Mathematica (1910) is considered a foundational work of the analytic tradition.

Moritz Schlick (1882–1936) was a German physicist and philosopher. Known primarily for his contribution to the field of logical positivism, he was a founding member of the Vienna Circle.

Adam Smith (1723–90) is the moral and political philosopher generally credited as the father of modern economics. His two most famous works are *The Theory of Moral Sentiments* (1759) and *An Inquiry into the Nature and Causes of the Wealth of Nations* (1776).

Socrates (469–399 B.C.E.) was an ancient Greek philosopher and one of the founding fathers of Western philosophy. His work is mostly known thanks to Plato's discussion of him, since little of his original work survived.

Baruch Spinoza (1632–77) was a major philosopher of the early modern period; he is noted for his contributions to metaphysics and philosophy of religion. Famous works include Ethics (1677) and Theological-Political Treatise (1670).

Bishop Samuel Wilberforce (1805–73) was an English bishop, best remembered today for his contribution to a famous debate with Thomas Huxley in 1860 on the subject of Darwinian evolutionary theory, to which he was opposed.

Ludwig Wittgenstein (1889–1951) was an Austrian philosopher who worked in Britain, making major contributions to the development of the school of analytic philosophy. His most famous works are the Tractatus Logico-Philosophicus (1921) and Philosophical Investigations (1953).

WORKS CITED

WORKS CITED

Blackburn, S. *How to Read Hume*. London: Granta Books, 2008.

Interview by Nigel Warburton, *fivebooks.com*, July 8, 2013, http://fivebooks.com/interviews/simon-blackburn-on-david-hume.

Bourget, D., and D. J. Chalmers. "What Do Philosophers Believe?" *Philosophical Studies* 170 (2014): 465–500.

Broadie, A. "Scottish Philosophy in the 18th Century." In *The Stanford Encyclopedia of Philosophy,* edited by Edward N. Zalta. Stanford: Metaphysics Research Lab CSLI, 2013, http://plato.stanford.edu/archives/fall2013/entries/scottish-18th/.

Butler, R. J. "Natural Belief and the Enigma of Hume." *Archiv für die Geschichte der Philosophie* 42 (1960): 73–100.

Coleman, D. (Ed.) *Hume: Dialogues Concerning Natural Religion and Other Writings*. Cambridge: Cambridge University Press, 2007.

Dennett, D. *Breaking the Spell: Religion as a Natural Phenomenon*. London: Penguin, 2006.

Dixon, T. *Science and Religion: A Very Short Introduction*. Oxford: Oxford University Press, 2008.

Fieser, J. *Early Responses to Hume's Life and Reputation*, vols 9 and 10. London: Bloomsbury, 2003.

Forrest, P. "The Epistemology of Religion." In *The Stanford Encyclopedia of Philosophy, edited by* Edward N. Zalta (Stanford: Metaphysics *Research Lab CSLI,* 2014), http://plato.stanford.edu/archives/spr2014/entries/religion-epistemology/.

Gaskin, J. C. A. "Hume on Religion." In *The Cambridge Companion to Hume*, edited by David Fate Norton. Cambridge: Cambridge University Press, 1993.

Glock, Hans-Johann. *What is Analytic Philosophy?* Cambridge: Cambridge University Press, 2008.

Hobbes, T. *Leviathan*, edited by C. B. Macpherson. London: Penguin Books, 1985.

Hume, D. *Dialogues Concerning Natural Religion*, edited by Stanley Tweyman. London: Routledge, 1991.

An Enquiry Concerning Human Understanding, edited by Tom L. Beauchamp. Oxford: Oxford University Press, 1999.

An Enquiry Concerning the Principles of Morals, new ed. Oxford: Oxford University Press, 1998.

Essays and Treatises on Several Subjects, vols 1–4. London: Adamant Media Corporation, 2000.

Four dissertations. I: The Natural History of Religion. II: Of the Passions. III: Of Tragedy. IV: Of the Standard of Taste. Michigan: Gale ECCO Print Editions, 2010.

The Letters of David Hume, vols I and II, edited by J. Y. T. Greig. Oxford: Clarendon Press, 1932.

"Natural History of Religion." In *Four Dissertations*. London: A. Millar, 1757.

A Treatise of Human Nature. USA: Andesite Press, 2015.

Hutchison Stirling, James. *The Secret of Hegel: Being the Hegelian System in Origin, Principle, Form, and Matter*. Charleston: BiblioBazaar, 2009.

Kant, I. *Critique of Pure Reason*, translated by N. Kemp Smith. London: Macmillan, 1976.

Religion within the Boundaries of Mere Reason, translated and edited by Allen Wood and George Di Giovanni. Cambridge: Cambridge University Press, 1998.

Konstan, D. "Epicurus." In *The Stanford Encyclopedia of Philosophy,* edited by Edward N. Zalta. Stanford: Metaphysics *Research Lab CSLI,* 2014, http://plato.stanford.edu/archives/sum2014/entries/epicurus/.

Markie, P. "Rationalism vs. Empiricism." In *The Stanford Encyclopedia of Philosophy,* edited by Edward N. Zalta. Stanford: Metaphysics *Research Lab CSLI,* 2015, http://plato.stanford.edu/archives/sum2015/entries/rationalism-empiricism/.

Mason, Richard. *The God of Spinoza: A Philosophical Study*. Cambridge: Cambridge University Press, 2010.

Mill, J. S. *Three Essays on Religion*. Bristol: Thoemmes Press, 1993.

Morris, W. E., and C. R. Brown, "David Hume," in *The Stanford Encyclopedia of Philosophy*, ed. Edward N. Zalta. Stanford: Metaphysics *Research Lab CSLI,* 2014, http://plato.stanford.edu/archives/sum2014/entries/hume/.

Mossner, E. C. *The Life of David Hume*, 2nd ed. Oxford: Oxford University Press, 2001.

Nadler, Steven. "Baruch Spinoza." In *The Stanford Encyclopedia of Philosophy,* edited by Edward N. Zalta. Stanford: Metaphysics *Research Lab CSLI,* 2013, http://plato.stanford.edu/archives/fall2013/entries/spinoza/, § 2.1.

Paley, W. *Natural Theology: Or Evidences of the Existence and Attributes of the Deity Collected from the Appearances of Nature.* Boston: Gould and Lincoln, 1867.

Penelhum, Terence. *David Hume: An Introduction to his Philosophical System.* West Lafayette: Purdue University Press, 1992.

Priestman, M. *Romantic Atheism: Poetry and Freethought, 1780–1830.* Cambridge: Cambridge University Press, 2007.

Pyle, A. *Hume's 'Dialogues Concerning Natural Religion': Reader's Guide.* London: Continuum, 2006.

Reichenbach, B. "Cosmological Argument." In *The Stanford Encyclopedia of Philosophy,* edited by Edward N. Zalta. Stanford: Metaphysics *Research Lab CSLI,* 2013, http://plato.stanford.edu/archives/spr2013/entries/cosmological-argument/.

Russell, P. "Hume on Religion." In *The Stanford Encyclopedia of Philosophy,* edited by Edward N. Zalta. Stanford: Metaphysics *Research Lab CSLI,* 2014, http://plato.stanford.edu/archives/win2014/entries/hume-religion/.

Schwartz, S. P. *A Brief History of Analytic Philosophy.* London: Wiley-Blackwell, 2012.

Scottish Television News. "Almost Half of Scots Not Religious, According to New Figures." August 26, 2015, http://news.stv.tv/scotland/1327477-almost-half-of-scots-not-religious-according-to-scottish-household-survey/.

Sessions, William Lad. *Reading Hume's Dialogues: A Veneration for True Religion.* Bloomington: Indiana University Press, 2002.

Springborg, P. "Hobbes's Challenge to Descartes, Bramhall and Boyle: A Corporeal God." *British Journal for the History of Philosophy* 20 (2012): 903–34.

Taliaferro, C., and E. J. Marty (Eds). *A Dictionary of Philosophy of Religion.* New York: Continuum, 2010.

Taylor, J. E. "The New Atheists." In *The Internet Encyclopedia of Philosophy,* edited by J. Fieser and B. Dowden (2015), http://www.iep.utm.edu/n-atheis/.

Tweyman, S. *Hume on Natural Religion.* London: Bloomsbury, 1996.

Scepticism and Belief in Hume's Dialogues Concerning Natural Religion. Dordrecht: Kluwer, 1981.

Warren, J. *Facing Death: Epicurus and his Critics.* Cambridge: Cambridge University Press, 2004.

THE MACAT LIBRARY
BY DISCIPLINE

The Macat Library By Discipline

AFRICANA STUDIES

Chinua Achebe's *An Image of Africa: Racism in Conrad's Heart of Darkness*
W. E. B. Du Bois's *The Souls of Black Folk*
Zora Neale Huston's *Characteristics of Negro Expression*
Martin Luther King Jr's *Why We Can't Wait*
Toni Morrison's *Playing in the Dark: Whiteness in the American Literary Imagination*

ANTHROPOLOGY

Arjun Appadurai's *Modernity at Large: Cultural Dimensions of Globalisation*
Philippe Ariès's *Centuries of Childhood*
Franz Boas's *Race, Language and Culture*
Kim Chan & Renée Mauborgne's *Blue Ocean Strategy*
Jared Diamond's *Guns, Germs & Steel: the Fate of Human Societies*
Jared Diamond's *Collapse: How Societies Choose to Fail or Survive*
E. E. Evans-Pritchard's *Witchcraft, Oracles and Magic Among the Azande*
James Ferguson's *The Anti-Politics Machine*
Clifford Geertz's *The Interpretation of Cultures*
David Graeber's *Debt: the First 5000 Years*
Karen Ho's *Liquidated: An Ethnography of Wall Street*
Geert Hofstede's *Culture's Consequences: Comparing Values, Behaviors, Institutes and Organizations across Nations*
Claude Lévi-Strauss's *Structural Anthropology*
Jay Macleod's *Ain't No Makin' It: Aspirations and Attainment in a Low-Income Neighborhood*
Saba Mahmood's *The Politics of Piety: The Islamic Revival and the Feminist Subject*
Marcel Mauss's *The Gift*

BUSINESS

Jean Lave & Etienne Wenger's *Situated Learning*
Theodore Levitt's *Marketing Myopia*
Burton G. Malkiel's *A Random Walk Down Wall Street*
Douglas McGregor's *The Human Side of Enterprise*
Michael Porter's *Competitive Strategy: Creating and Sustaining Superior Performance*
John Kotter's *Leading Change*
C. K. Prahalad & Gary Hamel's *The Core Competence of the Corporation*

CRIMINOLOGY

Michelle Alexander's *The New Jim Crow: Mass Incarceration in the Age of Colorblindness*
Michael R. Gottfredson & Travis Hirschi's *A General Theory of Crime*
Richard Herrnstein & Charles A. Murray's *The Bell Curve: Intelligence and Class Structure in American Life*
Elizabeth Loftus's *Eyewitness Testimony*
Jay Macleod's *Ain't No Makin' It: Aspirations and Attainment in a Low-Income Neighborhood*
Philip Zimbardo's *The Lucifer Effect*

ECONOMICS

Janet Abu-Lughod's *Before European Hegemony*
Ha-Joon Chang's *Kicking Away the Ladder*
David Brion Davis's *The Problem of Slavery in the Age of Revolution*
Milton Friedman's *The Role of Monetary Policy*
Milton Friedman's *Capitalism and Freedom*
David Graeber's *Debt: the First 5000 Years*
Friedrich Hayek's *The Road to Serfdom*
Karen Ho's *Liquidated: An Ethnography of Wall Street*

John Maynard Keynes's *The General Theory of Employment, Interest and Money*
Charles P. Kindleberger's *Manias, Panics and Crashes*
Robert Lucas's *Why Doesn't Capital Flow from Rich to Poor Countries?*
Burton G. Malkiel's *A Random Walk Down Wall Street*
Thomas Robert Malthus's *An Essay on the Principle of Population*
Karl Marx's *Capital*
Thomas Piketty's *Capital in the Twenty-First Century*
Amartya Sen's *Development as Freedom*
Adam Smith's *The Wealth of Nations*
Nassim Nicholas Taleb's *The Black Swan: The Impact of the Highly Improbable*
Amos Tversky's & Daniel Kahneman's *Judgment under Uncertainty: Heuristics and Biases*
Mahbub Ul Haq's *Reflections on Human Development*
Max Weber's *The Protestant Ethic and the Spirit of Capitalism*

FEMINISM AND GENDER STUDIES

Judith Butler's *Gender Trouble*
Simone De Beauvoir's *The Second Sex*
Michel Foucault's *History of Sexuality*
Betty Friedan's *The Feminine Mystique*
Saba Mahmood's *The Politics of Piety: The Islamic Revival and the Feminist Subject*
Joan Wallach Scott's *Gender and the Politics of History*
Mary Wollstonecraft's *A Vindication of the Rights of Woman*
Virginia Woolf's *A Room of One's Own*

GEOGRAPHY

The Brundtland Report's *Our Common Future*
Rachel Carson's *Silent Spring*
Charles Darwin's *On the Origin of Species*
James Ferguson's *The Anti-Politics Machine*
Jane Jacobs's *The Death and Life of Great American Cities*
James Lovelock's *Gaia: A New Look at Life on Earth*
Amartya Sen's *Development as Freedom*
Mathis Wackernagel & William Rees's *Our Ecological Footprint*

HISTORY

Janet Abu-Lughod's *Before European Hegemony*
Benedict Anderson's *Imagined Communities*
Bernard Bailyn's *The Ideological Origins of the American Revolution*
Hanna Batatu's *The Old Social Classes And The Revolutionary Movements Of Iraq*
Christopher Browning's *Ordinary Men: Reserve Police Batallion 101 and the Final Solution in Poland*
Edmund Burke's *Reflections on the Revolution in France*
William Cronon's *Nature's Metropolis: Chicago And The Great West*
Alfred W. Crosby's *The Columbian Exchange*
Hamid Dabashi's *Iran: A People Interrupted*
David Brion Davis's *The Problem of Slavery in the Age of Revolution*
Nathalie Zemon Davis's *The Return of Martin Guerre*
Jared Diamond's *Guns, Germs & Steel: the Fate of Human Societies*
Frank Dikotter's *Mao's Great Famine*
John W Dower's *War Without Mercy: Race And Power In The Pacific War*
W. E. B. Du Bois's *The Souls of Black Folk*
Richard J. Evans's *In Defence of History*
Lucien Febvre's *The Problem of Unbelief in the 16th Century*
Sheila Fitzpatrick's *Everyday Stalinism*

The Macat Library By Discipline

Eric Foner's *Reconstruction: America's Unfinished Revolution, 1863-1877*
Michel Foucault's *Discipline and Punish*
Michel Foucault's *History of Sexuality*
Francis Fukuyama's *The End of History and the Last Man*
John Lewis Gaddis's *We Now Know: Rethinking Cold War History*
Ernest Gellner's *Nations and Nationalism*
Eugene Genovese's *Roll, Jordan, Roll: The World the Slaves Made*
Carlo Ginzburg's *The Night Battles*
Daniel Goldhagen's *Hitler's Willing Executioners*
Jack Goldstone's *Revolution and Rebellion in the Early Modern World*
Antonio Gramsci's *The Prison Notebooks*
Alexander Hamilton, John Jay & James Madison's *The Federalist Papers*
Christopher Hill's *The World Turned Upside Down*
Carole Hillenbrand's *The Crusades: Islamic Perspectives*
Thomas Hobbes's *Leviathan*
Eric Hobsbawm's *The Age Of Revolution*
John A. Hobson's *Imperialism: A Study*
Albert Hourani's *History of the Arab Peoples*
Samuel P. Huntington's *The Clash of Civilizations and the Remaking of World Order*
C. L. R. James's *The Black Jacobins*
Tony Judt's *Postwar: A History of Europe Since 1945*
Ernst Kantorowicz's *The King's Two Bodies: A Study in Medieval Political Theology*
Paul Kennedy's *The Rise and Fall of the Great Powers*
Ian Kershaw's *The "Hitler Myth": Image and Reality in the Third Reich*
John Maynard Keynes's *The General Theory of Employment, Interest and Money*
Charles P. Kindleberger's *Manias, Panics and Crashes*
Martin Luther King Jr's *Why We Can't Wait*
Henry Kissinger's *World Order: Reflections on the Character of Nations and the Course of History*
Thomas Kuhn's *The Structure of Scientific Revolutions*
Georges Lefebvre's *The Coming of the French Revolution*
John Locke's *Two Treatises of Government*
Niccolò Machiavelli's *The Prince*
Thomas Robert Malthus's *An Essay on the Principle of Population*
Mahmood Mamdani's *Citizen and Subject: Contemporary Africa And The Legacy Of Late Colonialism*
Karl Marx's *Capital*
Stanley Milgram's *Obedience to Authority*
John Stuart Mill's *On Liberty*
Thomas Paine's *Common Sense*
Thomas Paine's *Rights of Man*
Geoffrey Parker's *Global Crisis: War, Climate Change and Catastrophe in the Seventeenth Century*
Jonathan Riley-Smith's *The First Crusade and the Idea of Crusading*
Jean-Jacques Rousseau's *The Social Contract*
Joan Wallach Scott's *Gender and the Politics of History*
Theda Skocpol's *States and Social Revolutions*
Adam Smith's *The Wealth of Nations*
Timothy Snyder's *Bloodlands: Europe Between Hitler and Stalin*
Sun Tzu's *The Art of War*
Keith Thomas's *Religion and the Decline of Magic*
Thucydides's *The History of the Peloponnesian War*
Frederick Jackson Turner's *The Significance of the Frontier in American History*
Odd Arne Westad's *The Global Cold War: Third World Interventions And The Making Of Our Times*

LITERATURE

Chinua Achebe's *An Image of Africa: Racism in Conrad's Heart of Darkness*
Roland Barthes's *Mythologies*
Homi K. Bhabha's *The Location of Culture*
Judith Butler's *Gender Trouble*
Simone De Beauvoir's *The Second Sex*
Ferdinand De Saussure's *Course in General Linguistics*
T. S. Eliot's *The Sacred Wood: Essays on Poetry and Criticism*
Zora Neale Huston's *Characteristics of Negro Expression*
Toni Morrison's *Playing in the Dark: Whiteness in the American Literary Imagination*
Edward Said's *Orientalism*
Gayatri Chakravorty Spivak's *Can the Subaltern Speak?*
Mary Wollstonecraft's *A Vindication of the Rights of Women*
Virginia Woolf's *A Room of One's Own*

PHILOSOPHY

Elizabeth Anscombe's *Modern Moral Philosophy*
Hannah Arendt's *The Human Condition*
Aristotle's *Metaphysics*
Aristotle's *Nicomachean Ethics*
Edmund Gettier's *Is Justified True Belief Knowledge?*
Georg Wilhelm Friedrich Hegel's *Phenomenology of Spirit*
David Hume's *Dialogues Concerning Natural Religion*
David Hume's *The Enquiry for Human Understanding*
Immanuel Kant's *Religion within the Boundaries of Mere Reason*
Immanuel Kant's *Critique of Pure Reason*
Søren Kierkegaard's *The Sickness Unto Death*
Søren Kierkegaard's *Fear and Trembling*
C. S. Lewis's *The Abolition of Man*
Alasdair MacIntyre's *After Virtue*
Marcus Aurelius's *Meditations*
Friedrich Nietzsche's *On the Genealogy of Morality*
Friedrich Nietzsche's *Beyond Good and Evil*
Plato's *Republic*
Plato's *Symposium*
Jean-Jacques Rousseau's *The Social Contract*
Gilbert Ryle's *The Concept of Mind*
Baruch Spinoza's *Ethics*
Sun Tzu's *The Art of War*
Ludwig Wittgenstein's *Philosophical Investigations*

POLITICS

Benedict Anderson's *Imagined Communities*
Aristotle's *Politics*
Bernard Bailyn's *The Ideological Origins of the American Revolution*
Edmund Burke's *Reflections on the Revolution in France*
John C. Calhoun's *A Disquisition on Government*
Ha-Joon Chang's *Kicking Away the Ladder*
Hamid Dabashi's *Iran: A People Interrupted*
Hamid Dabashi's *Theology of Discontent: The Ideological Foundation of the Islamic Revolution in Iran*
Robert Dahl's *Democracy and its Critics*
Robert Dahl's *Who Governs?*
David Brion Davis's *The Problem of Slavery in the Age of Revolution*

The Macat Library By Discipline

Alexis De Tocqueville's *Democracy in America*
James Ferguson's *The Anti-Politics Machine*
Frank Dikotter's *Mao's Great Famine*
Sheila Fitzpatrick's *Everyday Stalinism*
Eric Foner's *Reconstruction: America's Unfinished Revolution, 1863-1877*
Milton Friedman's *Capitalism and Freedom*
Francis Fukuyama's *The End of History and the Last Man*
John Lewis Gaddis's *We Now Know: Rethinking Cold War History*
Ernest Gellner's *Nations and Nationalism*
David Graeber's *Debt: the First 5000 Years*
Antonio Gramsci's *The Prison Notebooks*
Alexander Hamilton, John Jay & James Madison's *The Federalist Papers*
Friedrich Hayek's *The Road to Serfdom*
Christopher Hill's *The World Turned Upside Down*
Thomas Hobbes's *Leviathan*
John A. Hobson's *Imperialism: A Study*
Samuel P. Huntington's *The Clash of Civilizations and the Remaking of World Order*
Tony Judt's *Postwar: A History of Europe Since 1945*
David C. Kang's *China Rising: Peace, Power and Order in East Asia*
Paul Kennedy's *The Rise and Fall of Great Powers*
Robert Keohane's *After Hegemony*
Martin Luther King Jr.'s *Why We Can't Wait*
Henry Kissinger's *World Order: Reflections on the Character of Nations and the Course of History*
John Locke's *Two Treatises of Government*
Niccolò Machiavelli's *The Prince*
Thomas Robert Malthus's *An Essay on the Principle of Population*
Mahmood Mamdani's *Citizen and Subject: Contemporary Africa And The Legacy Of Late Colonialism*
Karl Marx's *Capital*
John Stuart Mill's *On Liberty*
John Stuart Mill's *Utilitarianism*
Hans Morgenthau's *Politics Among Nations*
Thomas Paine's *Common Sense*
Thomas Paine's *Rights of Man*
Thomas Piketty's *Capital in the Twenty-First Century*
Robert D. Putman's *Bowling Alone*
John Rawls's *Theory of Justice*
Jean-Jacques Rousseau's *The Social Contract*
Theda Skocpol's *States and Social Revolutions*
Adam Smith's *The Wealth of Nations*
Sun Tzu's *The Art of War*
Henry David Thoreau's *Civil Disobedience*
Thucydides's *The History of the Peloponnesian War*
Kenneth Waltz's *Theory of International Politics*
Max Weber's *Politics as a Vocation*
Odd Arne Westad's *The Global Cold War: Third World Interventions And The Making Of Our Times*

POSTCOLONIAL STUDIES

Roland Barthes's *Mythologies*
Frantz Fanon's *Black Skin, White Masks*
Homi K. Bhabha's *The Location of Culture*
Gustavo Gutiérrez's *A Theology of Liberation*
Edward Said's *Orientalism*
Gayatri Chakravorty Spivak's *Can the Subaltern Speak?*

PSYCHOLOGY

Gordon Allport's *The Nature of Prejudice*
Alan Baddeley & Graham Hitch's *Aggression: A Social Learning Analysis*
Albert Bandura's *Aggression: A Social Learning Analysis*
Leon Festinger's *A Theory of Cognitive Dissonance*
Sigmund Freud's *The Interpretation of Dreams*
Betty Friedan's *The Feminine Mystique*
Michael R. Gottfredson & Travis Hirschi's *A General Theory of Crime*
Eric Hoffer's *The True Believer: Thoughts on the Nature of Mass Movements*
William James's *Principles of Psychology*
Elizabeth Loftus's *Eyewitness Testimony*
A. H. Maslow's *A Theory of Human Motivation*
Stanley Milgram's *Obedience to Authority*
Steven Pinker's *The Better Angels of Our Nature*
Oliver Sacks's *The Man Who Mistook His Wife For a Hat*
Richard Thaler & Cass Sunstein's *Nudge: Improving Decisions About Health, Wealth and Happiness*
Amos Tversky's *Judgment under Uncertainty: Heuristics and Biases*
Philip Zimbardo's *The Lucifer Effect*

SCIENCE

Rachel Carson's *Silent Spring*
William Cronon's *Nature's Metropolis: Chicago And The Great West*
Alfred W. Crosby's *The Columbian Exchange*
Charles Darwin's *On the Origin of Species*
Richard Dawkin's *The Selfish Gene*
Thomas Kuhn's *The Structure of Scientific Revolutions*
Geoffrey Parker's *Global Crisis: War, Climate Change and Catastrophe in the Seventeenth Century*
Mathis Wackernagel & William Rees's *Our Ecological Footprint*

SOCIOLOGY

Michelle Alexander's *The New Jim Crow: Mass Incarceration in the Age of Colorblindness*
Gordon Allport's *The Nature of Prejudice*
Albert Bandura's *Aggression: A Social Learning Analysis*
Hanna Batatu's *The Old Social Classes And The Revolutionary Movements Of Iraq*
Ha-Joon Chang's *Kicking Away the Ladder*
W. E. B. Du Bois's *The Souls of Black Folk*
Émile Durkheim's *On Suicide*
Frantz Fanon's *Black Skin, White Masks*
Frantz Fanon's *The Wretched of the Earth*
Eric Foner's *Reconstruction: America's Unfinished Revolution, 1863-1877*
Eugene Genovese's *Roll, Jordan, Roll: The World the Slaves Made*
Jack Goldstone's *Revolution and Rebellion in the Early Modern World*
Antonio Gramsci's *The Prison Notebooks*
Richard Herrnstein & Charles A Murray's *The Bell Curve: Intelligence and Class Structure in American Life*
Eric Hoffer's *The True Believer: Thoughts on the Nature of Mass Movements*
Jane Jacobs's *The Death and Life of Great American Cities*
Robert Lucas's *Why Doesn't Capital Flow from Rich to Poor Countries?*
Jay Macleod's *Ain't No Makin' It: Aspirations and Attainment in a Low Income Neighborhood*
Elaine May's *Homeward Bound: American Families in the Cold War Era*
Douglas McGregor's *The Human Side of Enterprise*
C. Wright Mills's *The Sociological Imagination*

Thomas Piketty's *Capital in the Twenty-First Century*
Robert D. Putman's *Bowling Alone*
David Riesman's *The Lonely Crowd: A Study of the Changing American Character*
Edward Said's *Orientalism*
Joan Wallach Scott's *Gender and the Politics of History*
Theda Skocpol's *States and Social Revolutions*
Max Weber's *The Protestant Ethic and the Spirit of Capitalism*

THEOLOGY

Augustine's *Confessions*
Benedict's *Rule of St Benedict*
Gustavo Gutiérrez's *A Theology of Liberation*
Carole Hillenbrand's *The Crusades: Islamic Perspectives*
David Hume's *Dialogues Concerning Natural Religion*
Immanuel Kant's *Religion within the Boundaries of Mere Reason*
Ernst Kantorowicz's *The King's Two Bodies: A Study in Medieval Political Theology*
Søren Kierkegaard's *The Sickness Unto Death*
C. S. Lewis's *The Abolition of Man*
Saba Mahmood's *The Politics of Piety: The Islamic Revival and the Feminist Subject*
Baruch Spinoza's *Ethics*
Keith Thomas's *Religion and the Decline of Magic*

COMING SOON

Chris Argyris's *The Individual and the Organisation*
Seyla Benhabib's *The Rights of Others*
Walter Benjamin's *The Work Of Art in the Age of Mechanical Reproduction*
John Berger's *Ways of Seeing*
Pierre Bourdieu's *Outline of a Theory of Practice*
Mary Douglas's *Purity and Danger*
Roland Dworkin's *Taking Rights Seriously*
James G. March's *Exploration and Exploitation in Organisational Learning*
Ikujiro Nonaka's *A Dynamic Theory of Organizational Knowledge Creation*
Griselda Pollock's *Vision and Difference*
Amartya Sen's *Inequality Re-Examined*
Susan Sontag's *On Photography*
Yasser Tabbaa's *The Transformation of Islamic Art*
Ludwig von Mises's *Theory of Money and Credit*

Printed in the United States
by Baker & Taylor Publisher Services